EXISTENTIALISM AND
RELIGIOUS LIBERALISM

EXISTENTIALISM
and RELIGIOUS
LIBERALISM

By John F. Hayward

Beacon Press   Boston

*To the Perfect Receiver of every good
and imperfect gift*

PREFACE

This book grew out of a lecture invitation from the Minns Committee of the First Church and King's Chapel in Boston, administrators of the Thomas Minns Fund, established under the will of Susan Minns. The lectures were on the subject of existentialism and the liberal church. I am grateful to the Minns Committee for sponsoring the initial lectures and for encouraging the writing of the present volume. I wish also to thank the Beacon Press, especially Karl Hill and Claude Shostal, for their stimulating concern, their sympathetic criticisms of the manuscript, and their many helpful suggestions.

To my former teacher and colleague, Professor Charles Hartshorne, who gave me expert guidance in philosophy and theology "in the fullness of time," I owe a large debt not previously acknowledged. In the background of all my thinking and in the foreground of my affections, stands my former minister, teacher, one-time colleague at the University of Chicago, and continuing compatriot in the liberal ministry, Professor James Luther Adams. He is foremost among those cherished persons who have led me "to behold the beauty of the Lord, and to enquire in his temple."

CONTENTS

INTRODUCTION   I

PART ONE   *The Existentialist Challenge to Religious
            Liberalism*

  1. Sectarian Liberalism under Attack   7
  2. The Religious Impact of Existentialism   16
  3. Albert Camus and the Religious Liberal   28
  4. The Arena of Decision   40

PART TWO   *The Common Origins of Existentialism and
            Liberalism*

  5. The Melancholy and Rationalism of the Greeks   51
  6. The Covenant of Israel   64
  7. Biblical Crises of Faith   73
  8. Christian Affirmations   83

PART THREE   *Reform Liberalism*

  9. The Validity of Theological Language   93
  10. The Liberal Transmission of Tradition   105
  11. Worship in the Liberal Church   116

INDEX   128

INTRODUCTION

The religious liberal faces a persistent question: How can he be free from the authority of previous orthodoxies without rejecting all vital and sustaining connection with the past? Must freedom be linked with negation of faith and with spiritual emptiness? Does religious affirmation in traditional terms always imply bondage to orthodoxy? Liberal religious congregations and individuals cannot rally their forces indefinitely under the banner of denial. Yet corporate religious affirmation seems to move toward creedalism and threatens to bind the individual's freedom of decision.

When freedom is regarded as the center and substance of a religious institution, all else within that institution tends to be fluid and indistinguishable. It is just this restlessness of substance that is so trying to the liberal's peace of mind and to the cohesion of his churches. If he is truly liberal he must seriously entertain the steady procession of doubts and queries presented to him by the realities of his age. At the same time, as a human being, he needs that poise born of commitment and substantial affirmation characteristic of religious faith. Being in a church with others like himself, he can point to few or no common doctrines of religious substance which establish and unite the religious fellowship; there is only a community of method. Here, at least, he and his fellows are sure of themselves, unequivocally affirming that they are joined to preserve individual freedom of belief, a rational method of inquiry toward the truth, and a tolerance of all differing opinions.

The obverse side of the liberal's freedom in these respects is emptiness. He dreams of a more concrete and precise definition of his church, especially when asked by outsiders what his church affirms. Yet he dare not speak for anyone other than himself. This is not to say that the liberal's loyalty to his church is weak. Rather, he is at a loss to explain, to his own or his neighbor's satisfaction, precisely why his loyalty is so strong. The most striking mystery of his churchmanship is its strength, given its shifting ideational and symbolic base.

The mystery will remain as long as one understands the liberal church purely in terms of its method of free inquiry, without reference to any concrete religious substance. The analysis of any religious body, liberal or otherwise, demands that one distinguish between substance and method. "Substance" refers to a given body of attitudes, beliefs, and actions through which a religious group defines itself and its position. "Method" denotes the way in which a group proposes to preserve, refine, and reform its own substance.

Method is never independent of substance. What a man believes or what a group professes will determine the method of dealing with possible changes in personal belief or in corporate profession. Among religious liberals, "method" denotes the freedom of the individual or of a congregation to be openly critical of inherited forms of belief and practice and to make such new formulations, both positive and negative, as their own consciences and judgments require. This common faith in the method of freedom rests in turn on substantive attitudes toward the condition of man, attitudes which may or may not be conscious and explicit.

To understand the liberal church one must bring these underlying and constitutive attitudes to light. Otherwise, to say that one is a liberal because one believes in free inquiry and tolerance of differences is to fail to distinguish oneself from a large number of orthodox Christians and Jews, not to mention many existentialists. Even the most tradition-bound persons manage to pay homage to the principle of freedom which, along with honesty, love, courage, wisdom, sincerity, etc., are honored in ethical affirmations the world over. No successful organization, ecclesiastical or otherwise, is founded and perpetuated, much less expanded, on abstractions such as these. Liberal churchmen sometimes wonder why so few people join and support their churches, given the apparently universal appeal and relevance of liberal faith and action. Is not the answer to this question the fact that people are sluggish to support organizations which foster what they think they already have? To say "We believe in freedom" is like saying "We believe in courage." The would-be convert agrees, "So do I, and I don't need your church to sustain that belief." Only when the substance of faith that sustains the belief in freedom is made clear does a prospective church member begin to know whether or not he wants to join such a church.

One should not overlook the phenomenon of the free-minded man who is a refugee from religious orthodoxy, who still feels a need for "religion," and who welcomes membership in a liberal church which he can attend and still "believe what he likes." Permissive religion, like permissive education, or permissive methods of child-rearing, has a temporary appeal to anyone who feels that he has previously been restricted by an authoritarian system in his culture. But once the chains of bondage have been completely discarded, and once a second generation has been reared in the vacuum of freedom for its own sake, the question of the substance of faith is again brought forward. Or, if it is not, the liberal tends to drift away from the organization in which he achieved his freedom, just as a patient who is cured leaves the care of his doctor. Thus, some liberal churches come perilously close to making it their prime function to free man from the need for a church. There are liberals outside all church affiliation who might consider man's liberation from organized religion as the *only* legitimate function of the liberal church.

It is untrue to the genius of liberal religion to ignore its substance by preoccupying oneself solely with its method. The liberal theological revolutions in early nineteenth-century

America depended upon more than a vague fascination with freedom for its own sake. Previously men had believed that they were slaves to original sin and were justified only through the unmerited grace of God, but they later came to believe that their natures were honorable and worthy, that their motives were noble and their powers unlimited. On the foundation of this revolution in common belief, there was a new birth of the method of free inquiry. Men affirmed that they ought to be free because it is human nature to deserve freedom and to exercise it wisely.

This is not to say that religious liberalism has any monopoly on religious freedom. Protestant Christianity has its liberal wing in which the churches do not presume to bind their members to creedal affirmations. Even confessional Protestant churches have carried from the beginning some recognition of the ultimate value of the freedom of religious inquiry. Luther's dictum that every man must do his own believing as well as his own dying has stood as a perennial charter of religious freedom despite the long history of Protestant religious intolerance. Nevertheless, the openness of Protestant churchmen to self-reformation, wherever it exists, is founded upon a religious substance different from that of nineteenth-century American religious liberalism. Protestant Christianity affirms that God judges and redeems human life. Man is justified in the midst of his imperfections by God's grace. Freedom is not a natural endowment; it is a divine gift deriving from the loving initiative of the Almighty and overcoming the bondage of man's will to sinful compulsions. Man may wish to be free, but he is not actually free except by grace.

The religious liberal today, no less than his ancestors a century ago, is not readily attracted to the substance of classical Protestantism. He can hardly return to the point from which he has actively rebelled. He cherishes his own optimistic doctrine of the dignity and perfectibility of human nature. He has largely lost the Protestant realization of the bondage of the will and of freedom through grace. To the religious liberal Protestant creedalism appears to bind man's freedom of inquiry and action. When he is pushed to explain the religious substance underlying his faith in the method of freedom, he will have to confess his faith in man, his trust that human beings can, of their own wit and will, create the conditions of their own well-being.

Precisely at this point a far more serious question arises. In the modern era, man's faith in himself has been radically shaken. Man's confidence in his ability to create an ever more harmonious society has given way before the realities of personal anxiety and international savagery. And man's ingenuity has proven better adapted for destructive purposes than for nurturing his well-being. Civilization itself seems to be in the midst of decay. The expression and documentation of this trend has been given a disturbing eloquence in the literature, art and philosophy of existentialism. The sensitive liberal cannot remain unaffected. If formerly he was proud of being unencumbered by the baggage of old beliefs, now he must wonder whether he carries anything at all, or whether he is not perilously close to emptiness and its consequent despair. The image of human pathos has replaced the image of human nobility. Existentialist man demands freedom for himself, not because he believes he is capable of constantly progressing toward a more perfect society, but because he deserves the right of rebellion from an increasingly oppressive society. His sense for the overwhelming pathos of mankind drives the existentialist to cherish freedom: freedom from political tyranny and scientific mechanism; freedom from conventional prejudice and ideological system; freedom for fresh and unique decision, exercised anew in every moment of existence.

It is ironic that this new philosophical and religious substance embodied in the varieties of modern existentialism, this empty and foreboding estimation of the human condition, should provide powerful support for the liberal method of free action and free inquiry. The irony applies directly to the self-definitions of religious liberals. It is not sufficient to say that the liberal church depends on the gospel of freedom. We are driven to ask, "Freedom on what basis? On what religious substance?" When the existentialist replies, "On the grounds of human pathos," he challenges liberals to re-examine their faith in human nobility.

This book is written in response to the existentialist challenge, a response which is hopefully as sympathetic as it is critical. This book is written with the venturing faith that uncompromising freedom and genuine religious commitment are ultimately compatible. It is a testing of the faith that a man can be religiously disciplined and can also be free for self-reformation; that freedom does not exclude order or the giving of oneself to something that transcends the self.

The pages that follow reflect in part a liberal criticism of Christian orthodoxy. They also reflect a growing impatience among many liberals with a religion that is exclusively critical and therefore empty. The tendency to equate liberal religion with the denial of orthodoxy calls for the revival of the spirit of Schleiermacher's *Speeches of Religion to Its Cultured Despisers*. Everywhere religious liberals are growing weary of the emptiness of their own negations and are genuinely searching for grounds of faith more relative to their needs. To serve these needs in the face of the challenges of existentialism and with unbroken respect for human freedom of decision is the most pressing task for religious liberals today.

1. SECTARIAN LIBERALISM UNDER ATTACK

A body of common faith is implicit within religious liberalism and constitutes its inner religious substance. This faith has the potential to build a religious community, but it is threatened by certain changes of attitude among many serious-minded liberals. Existentialism in its more obvious and ultimate forms symbolizes and dramatizes that threat. Among religious liberals, elements of existentialism are beginning to be felt and to qualify the more classic substance of liberal faith.

What is the classic substance of liberal faith? To distinguish it from liberalism as the method of free inquiry, I shall call it "sectarian liberalism." Sectarian liberalism, when it is unimpaired by the assaults of existentialist elements, exhibits three characteristics: (1) religion is defined as a human achievement rather than a divine gift; (2) man is defined as naturally equipped to achieve all that is necessary for his well-being, including religion as one such achievement; (3) the function of freedom is to release that natural goodness of man which will lead all free men to live in spontaneous harmony and cooperation. Upon only a cursory study of these principles, one recognizes the lineaments of nineteenth-century religious liberalism. An analysis of the present-day bearing of these attitudes will reveal how much they are alive and active in American liberal religion even today. We shall turn to such an analysis, comparing classic sectarian liberalism with elements of challenge within Protestant Christianity and secular existentialism.

Sectarian religious liberalism is first an attitude toward religion itself. It says that religion is merely one facet of culture developed through the many instruments at man's command—through science and knowledge, through art and ritual, through education and nurture—but always through conscious *human* application, reasoning and control. Sectarian liberalism tends to assume that we agree upon ends (freedom, justice, truth, love, beauty, etc.) and should be preoccupied with the human means for achieving these ends. On the basis of this assumption, certain questions are constantly raised by liberal churchmen. They ask: "How can we get our message to more people?"—in their search for achievement in the realms of communication and propaganda; "How can we realize among ourselves a greater degree and sense of the community?"—as they seek for achievement in group dynamics and the sharing of insight; "How can we solve individual and social problems?"—with the usual liberal concern for achievement in personal living and political power and organization; "How can we become more self-aware?"—which reflects their desire for achievement in introspection and psychological health; "How can we make our worship services more vivid and meaningful?"—as they look for achievement in fashioning desired emotional-rational effects in group behavior. Religion becomes essentially a problem-solving activity undertaken by people who believe they are both obliged and equipped to render their own lives more meaningful. There is a distinctly heroic quality in this attitude toward religion and it bespeaks a heroic attitude toward life generally. The congregation gathers to pool its own resources for the improvement of life.

A fundamental element of Christianity has always stood in sharp contrast to this first attitude of sectarian liberalism. The Christian church is the body of those persons who believe they have been given from beyond themselves and beyond all their achievements a power and an assurance, a strength and a witness. They are assured that the Creator of heaven and earth is also the Redeemer of mankind, that what man most wants and needs—communion with his Maker and justification of his life in spite of its imperfections—has in fact been given to all mankind, and that the good news of the gift is mediated through the symbols, the practices, and the teachings of the church. This is not to say that religion is unconcerned with human achievement, but only that religion is essentially a gift, an initiative from God to man and not purely a human invention or achievement. Man is then under obligation to express the gift through his own cultural inventiveness and to bring culture more closely into line with the form and spirit of the gift. Man's achievements come in grateful response to the overwhelming wonder and uncontrived glory of God's gifts. Man is fulfilled because God acts, not because man possesses primary initiative.

In comparing sectarian liberalism with Christianity, we must not assume that the liberal feels no gratitude or sense of a divine gift. He may believe in God and in God's bounty. He is very apt to believe in nature and the goodness of nature. But all such gifts are seen as potential, not actual, as latent forces for man to turn into vital reality, if he only will. Therefore, by ethical heroism, by human kindness, by technical insight, man takes the raw materials of the natural world and fashions them into cultural values. Or, on a theistic level, man achieves by himself a righteousness which elicits, and thus "achieves," the blessing and peace of God. Thus, in sectarian liberalism, even the most pious liberal theism is a subtle brand of humanism. God rewards what man, by his heroic achievements, deserves.

Secular existentialism tends to agree with this first principle of sectarian liberalism. The existentialist would say, if there were any valid human religion, it would certainly be humanly achieved and in no way divinely given. But existentialism raises the question whether religion itself is a meaningful reality, or even a legitimate human function. This question moves us to examine the second major element in the substance of sectarian liberalism, namely, the liberal's belief that each person is born with the capacity to secure his total well-being through cooperative and communal living. Agreeing that religion is ideally a human achievement, the sectarian liberal goes on to assert that man can *in fact* achieve it.

Human capacity is here understood as primarily the intellectual powers. Man's capacity to know, while not infinite, is inexhaustible. Man can always advance beyond the given limits of his knowledge to a new level of knowing. Presupposed in this doctrine of man is a view of the world as indefinitely, though not infinitely, knowable. The world has sufficient inherent order to yield a relatively orderly account of itself through the operation of human intelligence. In spite of every error, there is no limit to the expansion of truth.

In addition to man's intellectual capacity to respond to the order of the world, he possesses other, more unique, powers of creativity by which he can make a world of his own. In church and state, home and family, art and science, men build up the structures of human ingenuity which, while not unrelated to the natural order, are in essence expressions of a peculiarly human order. Thus knowledge and creativity combine to produce the sectarian liberal's image of "the dignity of man." Even in man's most abject condition, even in his most disreputable abuses of his powers, the essential human capacity remains and never entirely loses its potentiality for creative reform and achievement. Success does not lie in the continual realization of "the dignity of man." It lies in man's indelible capacity to rise from defeat and in his never wholly lost hope of success. As such, he is worthy of tenderness and respect in his failures as well as in his achievements. His dignity is revealed in spite of, as well as because of, his behavior.

Existentialist thinking tends to diverge from this second element of sectarian liberalism. Man's vaunted capacity to know is negated by the unknowability of the world. Sectarian liberalism is heavily rationalistic in philosophical outlook, assuming some kind of correspondence theory of knowledge. Existentialism, like logical positivism, is distrustful of any presupposition of essential order in the world. "Essences," in the classic sense of ideational forms corresponding to the inherent structure of things, are in complete contrast to "Existence," the real, thick, other, opaque, "over-againstness" of the world as the existentialist sees it. The word "existentialism" is opposed to "essentialism" and exalts what *is* over what is *known*. The sectarian liberal's confidence that he can know and therefore largely control his own destiny is denied in existentialist thinking. In place of the liberal's heroic image of man is the existentialist's pathetic image of man. Man is primarily a sufferer inhabiting a reality he neither understands, nor controls, nor loves, nor trusts. His life is "pathos" and "passivity," not achievement and active control.

The obverse side of the existentialist sense of pathos is a kind of desperate creativity which resembles more closely the classic substance of sectarian liberalism. Man is pathetic; but he also is free. In his own free decisions, his authentic selfhood is revealed. If his world is meaningless, then his only hope for meaning lies in creative decision-making. To paraphrase Voltaire, "If there is no meaning, it is necessary to invent it." Thus a poignant element of heroism, lean and empty yet very muscular, enters into the existentialist pathos and establishes some contact with the liberal's faith in human creativity. But the contact is sporadic and easily broken, since the existentialist mind is obsessed with guilt and tragedy. The free decision of one individual affects another. The corporate decisions of men, tending to crush freedom and to destroy authentic selfhood, create compounded misery for mankind. Man has a guilty genius for torture and premature death. And death itself is the utter end to whatever faint glimmer of hope may exist in life.

Here existentialism has a curious affinity not with sectarian liberalism but with Christianity. The Christian view is that man's natural tendency (the existentialists would say "fate") is to exercise the freedom of his powers for destructive purposes as well as for constructive ones. In the light of the Christian faith, such ambiguities of motivation and consequence cause man's history to be a melancholy rise and fall of creation and destruction, were it not for the grace of God. In the Christian doctrine of redemption, one sees a striking departure from existentialist pathos. But the Christian doctrine of sin, treating the condition of man in his natural state, is not unlike the existentialist's pathetic image and quite in contrast to the sectarian liberal's heroic image.

The third major element in the classic substance of sectarian liberalism is the faith that as individual men become increasingly free, their society will become increasingly harmonious. The sectarian liberal delights in an essentially permissive approach to the behavior of religious groups. He is suspicious of the leadership of denominational authorities. He believes that experimentation within individual churches is as salutary for the growth of the denomination as the free expression and action of individual church members is for the development of single congregations. The permissive atmosphere is carried into all the major features of church life. In religious education the child is encouraged to articulate the ideas and values that begin to form in his own mind rather than assimilate a given religious heritage. It is even hoped that he will develop his own faith. If any of the data of historical faith are presented to the church school child, they are represented as options which can be freely rejected. The sectarian liberal church school teacher is rightly anxious lest his teaching become indoctrination. The child is not asked to absorb anything which is beyond his powers to choose freely. The teacher is required to try to relate ideas to the child's own experience, not only for the sake of communication and clarity, but also for the sake of presenting those alternatives of choice which the child, at his given age and maturity, is able to make in a conscious and deliberate fashion.

The possibility that such an approach to education is culturally irresponsible and an invitation to chaos is negated by the sectarian liberal's confidence that what the child natively and freely chooses will be beneficial to society, both to society at large and to the society of the church. The same confidence applies to the sectarian liberal's understanding of his own parish's corporate expressions of faith through worship. Group discussion emerges as the most nearly sacred form of church behavior. Many church school worship services are given the form of spontaneous, though guided, discussion. The professional habits and prerogatives of the ministry makes this possibility less likely for the regular adult Sunday morning service. However, the custom of "sermon talk-backs," consisting of a discussion of the sermon immediately after the service, has appeared in many liberal churches in the last fifteen years. The sermon itself is regarded primarily as a hypothesis—one man's study and opinion—which the individual members of church must examine, weigh, and test for themselves. A sermon which gives the impression of struggling through the complexities of an issue toward conclusions not yet solidified is apt to be better received than a sermon where conviction is bluntly stated, especially if that conviction arouses a counter opinion. Behind all these choices and preferences is the belief that society will flourish best if the individual feels absolutely free to decide all crucial issues according to the dictates of his own intellect and conscience. Free men who are thus exercising their internal freedom of decision and choice will live harmoniously together, for each will respect the other's freedom trusting that men are enough alike to select reasonably similar, integrating alternatives.

Such a doctrine of the church and society presupposes a belief in some kind of pre-established harmony and finds a precedent in the Enlightenment's faith in a universal moral and natural law. However, the contemporary sectarian liberal, responding to the prevailing tone of cultural relativism, is not apt to cite classical rationalism as the ground of his faith. He is not at all sure that the harmony of man is derived from the harmony of the spheres. He knows that freedom can easily lead to conflict, that men of equal good will can clash and become alienated beyond the reach of rational amelioration. Yet he trusts freedom because he trusts man. And he trusts man in spite of the opacity of the universe, God, nature, and all that makes up man's environment. His trust of man amounts to a kind of humanistic pre-established harmony.

Protestant and existentialist thought are equally critical of such a view of man. In Protestant thought, human freedom, man's dignifying but burdensome nemesis, is the source of both creativity and sin. And because of man's manifold anxieties and boundless pride, the sinful consequences tend to predominate unless individual men can submit to the guidance of God's judging and redeeming spirit. In terms of church doctrine this means that the Holy Spirit ultimately unites the church, not the free individualism of the members. It can be argued that these Protestant suspicions of unbridled freedom, when joined with the Protestant corporate religious sense, risk letting some kind of human authoritarianism in through the back door: what is interpreted as the will of God may be only an obvious clerical preference. But we cannot blink at the fact that intelligent, freedom-cherishing Protestants are suspicious of religious laissez faire and are looking for sources of social cohesion which neither violate nor depend exclusively upon individual choice.

The existentialist's analysis of the human situation is as preoccupied with the individual's freedom as the sectarian liberal's. But the existentialist is less sanguine about the fruits of freedom. He has seen man's extraordinary involvement in tragedy, an involvement which free action may increase rather than alleviate. But freedom is a kind of justification of humanity in spite of all the misery and hopelessness which its misuse causes. Therefore, since no social harmony, whether preestablished or achieved, is imputed in the existentialist diagnosis, this third article of sectarian liberalism is meaningless to existentialism. The method of freedom in the sense of a free decision-making process has acquired a supporting substance of belief other than its power to contribute to meaningful social structure. Moreover, just as the thrust for freedom in nineteenth-century religious liberalism contested the claims of Christian orthodoxy, now the concern for freedom of existentialist thinking is contesting the claims of the religious substance (shall we say "orthodoxy"?) of sectarian liberalism.

The lean, seemingly cynical and despairing view of man in modern secular existentialism should raise for every liberal serious questions about the nature of his own sectarianism. It does no good to try to cover the uneasiness arising from the existentialist challenge by crying forth ever more strident litanies on the Dignity of Man. The challenge must be entertained sympathetically, noting the possibility that existentialist elements have already entered into liberal thinking even without the liberal's full and conscious acknowledgment. The challenge may also be met by the help of any element of the liberal's Christian heritage which, in all freedom and good conscience, he can accept and integrate into his life. As was said earlier, liberals, Christians, and existentialists all unite in their respect for human freedom. It remains to be seen what each of these groups can contribute to one another toward reaching a faith that upholds, substantiates and gives life and growth to free men everywhere.

2. THE RELIGIOUS IMPACT OF EXISTENTIALISM

Existentialists are emerging today as potentially more apt for the guardianship of freedom than liberals. Their claims call for a sympathetic and careful examination. Theirs is not a single, identifiable, philosophic school. Its practitioners often disavow the label if only because they resist being classified in any type of philosophy. This fact is one of the essentially religious characteristics of existentialism. It is impatient of the specialized and technical inquiries which characterize university philosophy departments. It directs itself rather toward certain non-academic questions which are being peculiarly emphasized by the torturing dislocations of our times: the questions of anxiety and despair, sickness of mind and will, tyranny and war, and above all, the question of death. Organized religions, with their rituals, commandments and theological systems have traditionally claimed to deal with all such questions. These same matters are now being wrestled with by professional poets, novelists, artists, scholars and essayists who are as often outside the church as within it. Accordingly we should seek to identify the character of existentialism and its challenge to liberal religious faith not with a set of religious or philosophical doctrines but with a series of questions, doubts, and desperate hopes.

The peculiar resistance of existentialists to doctrine separates them not only from religious orthodoxy but also from every form of rationalism whether classical or scientific. Soren Kierkegaard, the most representative of all existentialist thinkers, directed some of his bitterest attacks against the rationalism of Hegel and, through Hegel, against the rationalistic presuppositions of all classical European philosophy back to the ancient Greeks. Kierkegaard's attack on the venerable tradition of classical rationalism makes it possible to define the meaning of the word "existentialism," as much as this nearly shapeless movement can be defined. "Existentialism," in contrast to "essentialism," affirms that being transcends thought, that existence transcends essence, that the immediate and experiential transcends the conceptual and universal. It is a reversal of Plato for whom "Essence" or "Idea" is richer in quality, in duration, and in the power of being than physical phenomena. For Plato, true reality must be discovered through reasoning rather than through perception. For Kierkegaard, such mental systems of meaning, conceptualizations or Essences, are manmade and are not capable of being tested in relation to any alleged fixed reality. Systematic thinking is man's pretense to affirm an absolute Truth. Actually it is no more than an elaborate ideological tool of human weakness or ambition, a tool designed either to protect oneself from harm or to inflict harm upon one's neighbor.

The essence of reality, which had seemed so ravishingly real and authoritative to Plato, to Hegel, and to all rationalists in the intervening period, is overwhelmingly opaque and unknowable to existentialism. This is not to say that existentialism is an anti-intellectual movement. It is anti-rational in the classical sense, but it has achieved this position through the most unrelenting use of the intellect. Both Kierkegaard and Nietzsche, who might be called the original existentialists in modern culture, "did not oppose reflection in order to annihilate it, but rather in order to overcome it by limitlessly engaging in it and mastering it." [1] They saw that it was man's fate to be continually trying to understand his existence. The word "continually" is the key. Our rational-scientific age can never rest in any decision, but must always annihilate the present state of thought and action in favor of an allegedly

[1] Karl Jaspers, *Reason and Existence,* trans. by William Earle, The Noonday Press, 1955, p. 32.

more precise understanding. As Kierkegaard said, "We live in a sea of reflection where no one can call to one another, where all buoys are dialectical." The increase in reason's effort to understand increases the sense of depth, darkness, and ultimate inscrutability in all there is to understand.

So far it is likely that most liberals would agree. They could assert with Jaspers that reason may be ever deceived in respect to details but that it must never doubt its own principle, its own pursuit of ideas in the interests of communication. However, the fierceness of the existentialist attack on rationalism derives from much more than the frustrations of philosophers who despair of discovering any irrefutable truths.

While liberals, Christians, and existentialists, might all agree that Being Itself is not discoverable by human understanding, they would differ in their conceptions of the religious efficacy of scientific truth. The liberal does not hesitate to apply the word truth to the best efforts of scientists and tends to anchor his religious and philosophical hopes in findings of science. Given the fact that scientific propositions are at best fragmentary, operational and capable of being superseded by later discoveries, they are nevertheless the truths by which men live and order their lives. However, Kierkegaard, who died as long ago as 1855, was suspicious of this religious use of science. He saw in science's tremendous potential for introducing order into the vagaries of human behavior a distinct threat to the meaningfulness of human life. The essence of that threat lies in transferring a binding structure of natural order to the human soul; and, being thus ravished by subhuman processes, man reduces himself to a trivial position in a huge, impersonal, and ultimately meaningless order of natural events. Kierkegaard was early suspicious of the dangers of dehumanization through science, technology and subsequent political orders. He respected the limited findings of the dawning science of his day, but not the pride of scientists who, with their little fragments of knowledge, thought they had found the key to human existence.

Kierkegaard's fears about the future of mankind under the oppression of technological and political ordering were echoed by Dostoevski. The Russian novelist's picture of the "Underground Man" is close to the agony and striving of modern existentialist images: here, man becomes disenchanted with the increasing organization of people through technology and politics, and proposes that the defense of human freedom must finally cause men to destroy the orders they have created in the name of enlightenment. This acute Russian saw that the urge to selfhood and freedom might drive a man toward anarchy, crime and violence rather than see himself submit to an unending encroachment of impersonal control over his behavior.

Dostoevski's romantic image of the rebel from underground who smashes the intellectual orders is less frightening to the existentialist mind than the modern image of man's reduction to a posthuman, antlike acceptance of absolute political authority. Jaspers acutely observes that, in the degree to which man believes himself to be an absolutely regular natural phenomenon (even though science may never be in total possession of the details), by so much does he render himself a species of animal, pointing toward a time when human history will come to an end in political absolutism.[2] Free will, a trait which distinguishes man most clearly from the rest of the animal kingdom, tends to be reserved only for that intellectual elite who are engaged in the endless task of finding the "proper" orders of human behavior. It is no accident that the greatest freedom found within totalitarian systems today is granted to men engaged in scientific and technological research, while those in the arts, where man's more native and radical freedom flourishes, are circumscribed.

Artists in democratic societies are not silent in the face of this continuing threat to their free activity. Jean-Paul Sartre sees man's perennial danger to be his failure to realize his own indelible freedom, and, by a certain misuse of freedom, to submit to oppressive order, and to allow himself to be bewitched by the multiform orders of religion, politics and rational systemization. In Sartre's *The Flies,* his retelling of the Greek drama of Electra and Orestes, he has a remarkable dialogue

[2] Jaspers, *op. cit.,* p. 87.

between Zeus and the murderous king of Argos, Aegistheus. The Argive king, surveying his years of tyranny, asks the king of the Gods, "Zeus, who am I? Am I anything more than the dread that others have of me?" Zeus replies in the affirmative and says sadly that he too has bewitched the world into dread of himself and has thus created order upon order superimposed on the freedom of men. "Their eyes are so intent on me that they forget to look into themselves." Nor is this tyranny of order anything Zeus or the earthly king can reject; they must uphold it eternally! So Aegistheus, who has murdered his predecessor and married the queen, confesses: "I have lived without love, without hope, even without lust. But I . . . have kept good order in my kingdom. That has been my ruling passion; a godlike passion, but how terrible!" To which Zeus replies, "We could have no other, you and I; I am a God and you were born to be king." Thus in one stroke Sartre shows how the whole history of Western man, ravished by the lure of the Absolute in religion, in politics, in human law, has ever practiced the terrible art of tyranny.

Sartre is obsessed with the paradox that every man demands freedom for himself, and at the same time, can understand and treat every other man only as "thing," an object to be manipulated. Each man comes to be known as a waiter, or a Jew, a criminal, or a businessman, etc., ad infinitum—all men having distinct roles and classifications through which they must suffer manipulation and control. This is the background of Sartre's famous definition of Hell appearing at the end of his play, *No Exit:* 'There is no need for red-hot pokers: Hell—is other people."

The hell that other people provide is the terrible unresolved tension one must feel between the inner drive for freedom and the fact that, in taking decisive action, one compromises his own and other men's freedom by the imposition of objective order. If such order had a believable universal sanction, it could be tolerated or even loved. But all such sanctions are illusory. In the face of the utter inscrutability and meaninglessness of anything which is presumed to constitute Reality Itself, men must invent meanings and impose these invented meanings on others. Men are driven to objectify, judge, and punish human beings and, at the same time, to see the ultimate meaninglessness of what they are driven to do. As Sartre says: "Man, with no support and no aid, is condemned every moment, to invent man." [3]

In short, the burden of freedom is too great. As Camus has indicated in his novel, *The Fall*, instead of being internally free and granting others the freedom to decide on meanings and values immediately and freshly, we maintain among one another systems of rules, sins, and punishments. In our day, atheists administer this system of sin and punishment formerly maintained by the church; and they do so without the mitigating balm of grace.

How different are these outlooks from the sectarian liberal's notion that there is a basic harmony between himself, his brother, and his world which, when released through his own free action, will create an order among men closely analogous to the order of nature! For the liberal, freedom is the occasion for the appearance of meaningful order. For the existentialist, freedom is the occasion of anxiety, guilt, and pathos. From the existentialist's point of view, the liberal's preoccupation with man's scientific mastery of his world and his destiny partakes of the pretentiousness of both strains of rationalism: the classical and the scientific. The liberal world master, flinger of thunderbolts from the Olympus of the laboratory, is really a poor creature. His ingenuity is more suited to destruction than creation. His only dignity lies not in what he creates but in his power to resist the tyranny both of nature and of the monsters arising from his own technology. Dostoevsky's *Underground Man* is no Prometheus of the intellect; but he is forever impelled to overthrow every abstract system of human organization, no matter how utopian its effects may appear to be. Precisely from this wreck of the human image the existentialists seek to salvage the conviction that man's power of decision is the sole distinction of his humanity and justifies his existence in the midst of his meaninglessness. Sartre is the apostle of a desperate individuality utterly foreign to the

[3] Jean-Paul Sartre, *Existentialism*, Philosophical Library, 1947, p. 28.

calm celebration of man's spirit and his loving interrelatedness so common to the liberal witness.

Nearly one hundred and fifty years ago Francisco Goya anticipated Sartre's literary portraiture in his series of etchings, "The Disasters of the War." Goya documented in shocking detail the inhumanity of man to man, revealing with equal candor the atrocities of the French invaders and the crudely armed Spanish peasantry who arose to resist them. Through Goya's eyes we look into the utterly unromantic agonies of death's kingdom. And we see there also a faint glow of virtue, an ambiguous value shining darkly in the night: the power of men in all their wretchedness to affirm their lives and strength against the overwhelming power of death. To accept suffering and one's own weakness, to struggle for life, and to decide to be and to act without benefit of suprahuman support or supraindividual organization is truly characteristic of the existentialists' view of the human condition. The agony and dignity of man's life is summed up in the cry which Sartre puts into the mouth of Orestes who, defying Zeus to his face, says, "I *am* my freedom. No sooner had you created me than I ceased to be yours. . . . For I, Zeus, am a man, and every man must find out his own way. Nature abhors man, and you too, god of gods, abhor mankind."

These observations about existentialist thought leave a host of questions unanswered. There is the question of man's social nature, his deep dependence upon human love and the power that springs from loving relationships; the fact that man is also a cultural being who is ennobled as well as scarred by his historical heritage; the necessity to establish reasonable human relationships in spite of the ever present danger of an overly oppressive order. None of these problems is touched by the individualistic aspects of existentialism which we have been stressing. Our concern is not to defend or promote existentialist philosophy, but only to present clearly its challenge to sectarian liberalism. That challenge is most keenly felt in the question of the meaning and dignity of man's individuality. While the liberal sees man's free individuality as the occasion for his greatest creativity, his most meaningful cooperation, his most thoroughgoing righteousness, the existentialist sees in man's individual freedom an unavoidable condition of tragedy and pathos. It is just man's lonely individuality which is at once his sole dignity and his helpless abandonment. By his freedom he is a man; in the misuse of his freedom he has succeeded in endlessly violating what meager dignity he has ever possessed.

Some existentialists have felt that the only relief from the pathetic chaos of freedom lies in its relation to a transcendent reality that offers a meaningful choice without compromising the actual freedom to choose. Kierkegaard remained anchored in his own unique and astringent Christianity and from this basis condemned every other absolute including those abuses which, in his latter years, he believed he saw in the church. Jaspers contends that Nietzsche's respect for "sublime chance" comes close to what Kierkegaard understood as Providence and thereby shows that Nietzsche is nourished by a "pre-Socratic Hellenism." [4] Jaspers' own view of Being Itself is distinctly transcendent over and partly regulative of that which manifests itself as Being-for-me.[5] None of these references to the transcendent should be construed as relieving in any essential feature the loneliness of man, or his necessity to make his own choices in face of the ultimate mystery of his situation. The very austere demand of Self-subsistent Being is that man shall not destroy his own personal manifestation of that Being by being false to himself. Nor can a man know the majesty and ultimate peace of such Being until he has been disabused of all the fond dependencies which he once believed were the core of his existence. In his final loneliness he will know the solitary despair of the ultimate freedom of Being Itself.

In the foregoing forms of metaphysical existentialism one is aware of a transcendent Spirit or Something which seems to be lacking in Sartre's description of the utterly empty human situation. For Sartre, man is totally alone. He has no "human nature." Not even his aloneness will serve as a valuable or meaningful essence to share with his fellow men. Whatever a

[4] Jaspers, *Reason and Existence*, pp. 37, 43.
[5] *Ibid.*, pp. 58, 59.

man in his freedom chooses to assert tends to hurt his fellow men. Guilt follows upon freedom; pathos exists both with and without freedom. Sartre calls for "total engagement" in the worldwide struggle for freedom, but he avoids trying to prove that man can find any rational, essential meaning or value from such engagement. His consistent witness to human pathos finally merits the title of "nihilism"—he uses reason and human communication generally to destroy rationality and meaningfulness.

It is clear from what has been said that the substance of sectarian liberalism is not the sole way of supporting the reality of human freedom. The liberal's trust that a religion can be humanly fashioned to support man's dignity, that man has by nature the power to achieve an increasingly meaningful structure of values in cooperation with a benevolent reality, and finally, that free men acting in freedom will become progressively harmonious with one another—all come to utter shipwreck in existentialism's unrelenting picture of human bondage, guilt, anxiety, suffering and death. Sectarian liberalism descends from and is sustained by the Enlightenment's reinterpretations of Christian faith and hope. Sectarian liberalism is rationalistic through and through, giving to man reason and tolerance, those hopeful powers which once were thought to reside in God's providence and which are now located in human nature and in the relative tractability of the world to human control. By virtue of this religious substance, this celebration of the nobility and essential *competence* of man, the liberal asserts that each man deserves to be free. The contrasting religious substance of existentialism is like a secularized version of the classic Christian doctrine of original sin. Man is ridden with guilt and anxiety and is a pathetic incident momentarily caught in the ultimately supreme pressures of an unknown world. His only distinction, his major claim to be something more than nothing, is his freedom. This he *must* assert if he is to be in any way human. And in asserting freedom he and his fellows must inevitably suffer. He is free, not by virtue of his nobility, but by virtue of that desperation which must resist his own threatened nonentity. The liberal says that man is and must be free because he is so much more than his usual self-understanding. The existentialist says that man is and must be free because he is so much less than his usual self-understanding.

It may be that the history of nineteenth- and twentieth-century man has been so basically tragic that we must thank the existentialists for salvaging freedom even if they appear to have done so at the tremendous price of emptiness. At least freedom stands rescued from the long attrition and decline it has suffered in the modern world and perhaps it is waiting for a new and more fruitful assertion of its meaning and purpose. The lean and desperate condition of the existentialists' faith in freedom may not be easily apparent to those who dwell comfortably in the affluent society and who have been little or not at all touched by the shattering of European civilization through tyranny and war. But no sensitive citizen of the Western Hemisphere can fail to notice signs of decay in his own social structure and cultural resources, nor is the dawning disillusionment of the present time an absolutely new phenomenon. America, too, has had her prophets who have announced the coming of the present destructions and dislocations.

In nineteenth-century America the contrast in religious outlook between Ralph Waldo Emerson and Herman Melville prefigures the contrast between a sectarian liberal and a modern existentialist attitude. While Emerson was keenly aware of the reality of evil and the constant danger of man's self-degradation, he believed that the core of existence is essentially moral and beneficent, that man can lay hold of that core and by its powers transform his world ever nearer to the image of a transcendental virtue. Melville saw both beauty and savagery in all things, in man and in nature. But at the heart of existence, beyond beauty and savagery, he saw an ultimate mystery—an utter obliviousness to man and his needs. Here, irresistible power combines with a kind of unconscious or careless malignity to defy all human probings and destroy all human hopes. The great white whale in Melville's *Moby Dick* is his supreme symbol of the malignant dimension of ultimate being. It is man's fate, like that of the crew of the whaleship *Pequod,* to hunt the white whale in heroic opposition to suffering and death, to seek to slay him, and to be slain by him.

Thus the burgeoning technological and political civilization of nineteenth-century America looked different to Emerson than it did to Melville. Emerson trusted divinity and asked man to fashion his erring ways in tune with the Divine even as he was slowly conquering and rendering the harshness of a new continent into the service of human purposes. Melville distrusted all that lay outside man's province and much that lay within it. Yet he shared something of Emerson's sense for the heroic and conceived of his art as recording man's glorious yet hopeless fight to become the master of an essentially ungovernable existence. "I shall spread a rainbow over man's disastrous set of sun," Melville said. Like Kierkegaard and quite unlike Emerson, he was impatient with the pretenses of intellectual systems. But he did not succumb to a sense of man's utter pathos and insignificance characteristic of some modern existentialist philosophy and literature. Melville sensed the saving warmth of affection capable of arising between men and even saw it as religiously significant in contrast to the follies of traditional theology.

It is obvious that existentialist thinking has been preoccupied with a pathetic dynamic in modern society which is illustrated by the transition from Emerson through Melville to Sartre. The picture of the free man, beginning with the Age of Reason and supported by the great democratic political revolutions, is transformed into something very different by the titanic labors of modern technology to subdue the earth. Man emerges first as a tragic figure who fails grandly at a hopeless task and finally as a pathetic figure whose misery is only compounded by his weak and misbegotten strivings. The sectarian liberal in America has not been caught up in this passage of opinion from Promethean glory, through tragedy to pathos. He has remained faithful to the image of man's dignity, to his power "if he only will" to make of his world a paradise of justice and abundance.

The liberal who has shaken loose from these sectarian

moorings finds that his religious orientation is seriously threatened. His faith is undercut by the facts of world-wide tyrannies and wars, by the seemingly ineradicable plight of refugees and displaced persons, by the reigns of terror and the means of violence ever poised to destroy the uneasy truce across the face of hostile continents. The liberal is also embattled spiritually by the documentation and amplification of those horrors in painting and sculpture and in so many of the novels, plays, and poetry in current circulation. He cannot ignore the world-wide atmosphere of nihilism and despair or the equally desperate absolutisms which threaten to upset what little equilibrium the world still retains.

Thus two kinds of liberals find it difficult to understand each other: the man who is preoccupied with the achievements of rational, scientific man looks upon existentialist concerns as morbid; the man who has taken seriously the existentialists' unmasking of the sectarian liberal's grandiosity knows that he cannot return to that former optimism and dreads to occupy the empty spaces he sees before him. Yet as the philosopher, William Barrett, writing in defense of the relevance of existentialism has said, "We are all the Underground Man to some degree. He is that dark side of our being with which we must try to live in peace, and if we take lightly his fulminations against a human regime completely controlled by science and reason, we do so at our own risk." If there is to be a new liberalism, there must also be a renewed religious substance within it to sustain the freedom that all men cherish. Nor can the challenges of the most nihilistic forms of existentialism be overlooked or lightly set aside as irrelevant because of their seemingly morbid character. The liberal is equally subject, with all men, to an ancient canon of religious discipline: the way beyond crisis is not around it, but through it.

3. ALBERT CAMUS AND THE RELIGIOUS LIBERAL

The writings of Albert Camus are uniquely relevant to our inquiry because he embodies and, at the same time, transcends the existentialist pathos. No one has more eloquently expressed the nihilism and lonely individualism of modern European civilization than he. But even as he documents the breakdown of traditional human and religious values, he continues to transmit in altered form much that is religiously sustaining in Western culture. It is as though he had learned to appropriate the nourishment of his history while remaining free of it. He points the way beyond nihilism, but he does not advocate a return or explicit recourse either to sectarian liberalism or the Judeo-Christian tradition.

Camus' most nihilistic writing is to be found in his brief novel, *The Fall* (1956). This strikingly objective work does not advocate a philosophy of nihilism. It shows the devastating range and effects of nihilism; it confronts the reader with a picture of the personal suffering, moral depravity, and utter meaninglessness of a life which is wholly self-centered, unprincipled and unrelated. Even more striking than the final image of human nothingness is the author's account of its development. The main character, Clamence, tells the story in the first person to a chance acquaintance in an Amsterdam bar. Clamence is a former Parisian lawyer who in his learning, savoir faire, joie de vivre and above all, in his dedication to the use of his law practice for the relief of the poor, the widows and orphans, could be the model of humane liberalism. Clamence has no traditional religion, no conscious ideology, nor any protection of inherited wealth or personal privilege. He recalls a self-image of the glorious days of personal and professional success; he presents the picture of a man who has achieved a certain quintessential humanity "on his own."

The "fall" is Clamence's inner realization of the fact that his triumph is hollow and even despicable. Furthermore it is a fall without grace. In his fallen condition, he is in no way healed, but rather is driven to impute to all mankind a depravity similar to his own. He goes so far as to become a kind of high priest or, as he says, "Judge-Penitent" of mankind in its essential wickedness. His only "joy" is his satanic recognition of the reality of evil and his freedom from all obligation to oppose it or hope for its relief.

In the course of his self-disclosure, Clamence reveals that he enjoyed his work in the days of his confident liberalism because he could help his clients without being personally committed to them or without feeling in any way responsible for their suffering. He enjoyed his friends because they found him to be charming and desirable without requiring him to call on them or to make sacrifices in their behalf. He enjoyed his lovers because, in his "realism," he had learned when to abandon them, how not to be made captive by excessive affection or marriage. He even enjoyed the death of his friends because he could experience a generous outpouring of affection in their behalf without taking upon himself any further burden of commitment to their terminated reality. He enjoyed bodily health and sports but still could look forward to the less vigorous regimen of later years when he could be sustained by his concern for reading, conversation, and the arts.

> Thus I progressed on the surface of life, in the realm of words as it were, never in reality. All those books barely read, those friends barely loved, those cities barely visited, those women barely possessed! . . . Then came human beings; they wanted to cling but there was nothing to cling to, and that was unfortunate—for them. As for me, I forgot. I never remembered anything but myself.

Subsequent events narrated by Clamence in Camus' *The Fall* reveal how the main character discovers that he is a coward when his personal safety is threatened, that he is a tyrannical judge (and no longer an impartial defender of justice) when an injustice is done against him, and finally, that he sees himself and all men as anxious to be called innocent in the midst of their guilt. "In short, we should like, at the same time, to cease being guilty and yet not to make the effort of cleansing ourselves. . . . We lack the energy of evil as well as the energy of good."

From this state of disillusionment, to which a pretentious humanism is peculiarly susceptible, Clamence moves to his miserable role of "Judge-Penitent." He elicits from chance acquaintances at his favorite public bar a sympathetic hearing for his own confessions. Such confession leads his listeners to confess. Having first been penitent, he feels free to reverse his role and sit in smug and cruel judgment over the alleged enormity of all men's doings. Then, accepting the utter lack of objective standards and the utter hostility and evil in all men, he can go forth from his lay confessional and "sin" to his heart's content. Nor is there any real contentedness in his sinning or not sinning. He is convinced that it is natural for men to abuse and enslave one another. His only "satisfaction" is to have found a way of justifying himself for doing what is natural.

The epigraph of this biting novel quotes Lermontov as wishing to portray, in *A Hero of Our Time,* not an individual but "the aggregate of the vices of our whole generation in their fullest expression." One may suppose that Camus had the same purpose in writing *The Fall:* to show not only the extent of nihilism and its consequences in modern Europe but to show also how such a state of mankind could have developed out of unsuspected flaws in a confident, self-approving, liberal culture. It is clear that liberalism alone is not responsible for the thoroughgoing depravity documented in Camus' book. But any sensitive liberal reader cannot fail to be challenged by the peculiarly liberal virtues of Clamence as they are seen to be giving way to vice.

Any author who views society as it is described in *The Fall* will cause no surprise when he opens his book of essays, *The Myth of Sisyphus,* with the sentence, "There is but one truly serious philosophical problem and that is suicide." Beyond the obviously negative character of this sentence, Camus is asking, given the futilities and miseries of the modern world, how do we understand man's persistent drive for life, his constant refusal to resort to suicide? The question implies a powerful and positive religious drive. Man wants to find that meaning of life which is capable of surviving every condition of tragedy and pathos among men.

Camus finds that man is caught in the tension between two irreconcilable facts: the world yields no ultimate meaning to overcome its contradictions and miseries; yet human nature demands an order, a unity and a harmony to explain experience. The power of existence and man's drive toward lucidity will neither be denied nor reconciled. A total impression of absurdity without one lucid moment would automatically dictate suicide. But the drive for lucidity is as powerful as life itself, and will not yield to death even when the opacity and mystery of existence closes in. Camus is critical of those forms of existentialism represented by Jaspers and Kierkegaard which presume that there is an effective transcendent lucidity even though the human mind cannot grasp it. It is a contradiction of human experience to deify the absurdity of existence and claim that its heart is one and is pure, we know not how.

The mythological figure of Sisyphus gives Camus, in the early stages of his thinking and writing, his basic image of the human condition. The gods have punished Sisyphus in Hades by requiring him to push a great rock to a hilltop for eternity, with the provision that every time the rock is finally located at the top of the hill, it will roll down and Sisyphus' futile labor must begin all over again. So all men are born to give passionate effort to labors which will come to absolutely nothing. Whether in human relations, in art, or politics, we must achieve what our desire for unity and lucidity demands. But we must be prepared to see all our work and our lives come to naught. Camus observes a secret joy in Sisyphus, "One must

imagine Sisyphus happy." Such happiness stems from the recognition of the double fate of man: first, that as a man, he
has a task to achieve, and the power to achieve it; second, that
he knows his work has no meaning beyond himself, that he
is indebted to no one. Just as he cannot find any cosmic justification of his labor, so he needs fear no cosmic judgment over
his inadequacies. He is free of the transcendent, free to be
human and to be and do what he will in the midst of his
sufferings, in spite of death. He does not have to explain death;
he is free to live with an eye to life as long as death does not
claim him.

There is a strong note of Promethean defiance in *The
Myth of Sisyphus,* or, as Camus states it, "There is no fate
that can not be surmounted by scorn." There is also a prophetic
and religious depth in man's scornful rebellion against every
false claim to understand the ultimate meaning and obligation
of reality. Camus' sacred scorn is akin to the Old Testament
prophets' vigorous rejection of all human idols and every claim
to be or represent God. But the energy of protest among the
prophets sprang from the affirmation of a transcendent divine
meaning. Camus would criticize this assumption as surely as
he criticizes a similar attitude in Jaspers and Kierkegaard. Does
this mean that Camus is a total sceptic with respect to ultimate
values? Is a destructive nihilism the only possible consequence
of his outlook, as one might infer from the work of Sartre?

The later works of Camus wrestle with this alternative
and dismiss it as vigorously as dogmatic absolutism. Although
man can appeal to no transcendent destiny for the guidance of
his actions, he must struggle for his neighbor as well as for
himself against all that would cripple, thwart, or defeat humanity. He must struggle especially against the Ultimate Enemy,
Death, in what is obviously a losing battle. This struggle is not
conceived heroically. All men must eventually lose and whatever they achieve even in a temporary victory will by no means
conquer death or eradicate all human suffering. The figure of
Dr. Rieux in Camus' novel, *The Plague* (1947) most clearly
embodies this attitude. He speaks of "common decency" born
of sympathy as he sets about the hopeless task of attending to

the plague victims. "Heroism and sanctity do not really appeal to me, I imagine. What interests me," he says, "is being a man." This is a profoundly religious statement, in which the Sisyphus image of conquering one's fate by scorn, is deepened to include the achievement of sympathy and love. To be a man is to exert loving care and concern toward one's fellow human beings even as there seems to be no metaphysical or theological or ecclesiastical justification for such action.

The essentially non-heroic, non-Promethean element in this attitude lies in Camus' recognition that all the best-intentioned action in the world is ambiguous in value. Man does not act out of any clear knowledge of the good or any pure and untainted motivation. The plague of humanity besets all men, including the doctors seeking to cure it. "We can't stir a finger," says Jean Tarrou, another character in *The Plague,* "without the risk of bringing death to somebody." Our struggle with death is within ourselves as well as in the outer world. The struggle itself is unending for anyone who would assert his manhood; nor is there any final victory. We can deify no method whatsoever. Although the urge not to spread the plague may seem to dictate an absolute pacifism, there will be times when force will have to be employed. Above all, Camus avoids the temptation to say that humanity in itself represents any absolute value. He takes a somewhat paradoxical view of man. Whereas Clamence in *The Fall* moved from felicity and self-approval to misery and self-contempt, Rieux and Tarrou in *The Plague* move from near despair in their suffering to a new sense for human goodness. On the very last page of his novel the author has his narrator, Dr. Rieux, remark that the purpose of the chronicle is "to state quite simply what we learn in time of pestilence: that there are more things to admire in men than to despise." Especially in prolonged crisis, the decency of men is their only weapon against the tide of death within and outside them. It is not nobility, not "goodness" nor "dignity" in any unqualified sense. The expression of decency has to be found and trusted amid man's continuing baseness and futility.

Accordingly, Camus does not do away completely with

the value of scorn as celebrated in *The Myth of Sisyphus*. He transmutes mere scorn and anger toward the world or oneself into the image of rebellion for humanity's sake. His concept of rebellion includes within it the element of love. The quintessence of Camus' thought in this direction appeared in his long essay, published in 1951, called *The Rebel*. "Rebellion cannot exist without a strange form of love. Those who find no rest in God or in history are condemned to live for those who, like themselves, cannot live: in fact, for the humiliated." In this striking paradox Camus confesses that those who have no reason for living, no idol to worship, who almost literally cannot live because of their realization of the horror and futility in all lives, yet *do* live by compassion for one another. Having been humiliated by governments, religions, and ideologies, these rebels form a holy and compassionate brotherhood. Their rebellion is not merely protest. It is rather the attempt to use the heart and the intelligence toward finding temporary means beween extremes, toward resisting the absolute excesses of fanatical faith and fanatical nihilism by exercising a salutary relativism.

Camus represents a kind of revival of stoicism in his praise of moderation (*mésure*) which he calls, at the end of *The Rebel,* "Thought at the Meridian." There is a never-ending need for man to be aware of the corrupt tendencies within himself and to find a relative equilibrium between the absolutism of faith and the absolutism of scepticism. Rebellion is sacred when it is rebellion in behalf of the center, when "it does not triumph either in the impossible or in the abyss. It finds its equilibrium through them." Above all, man must recognize that no standard of *mésure* is given to him from beyond himself. This would be to yield, if ever so subtly, to the insidious temptation to absolutism. In this respect Camus is not a stoic in the classic sense: he does not invoke any transcendent natural or moral law. No man can make his decisions through any perspective which allegedly transcends history. He can only recognize the immediate excess and in the name of compassion and moderation, rebel against it. Each decision is relative to its times and runs the risk of being wrong or, what is much worse, injurious.

Camus acknowledges that all human decisions are a kind of "calculated culpability." Our opportunity is not to become more godlike by being right; it is to become more human by being less wrong.

Camus has brought forth from the excesses and negations of modern existentialism a chastened optimism, a clearly humane and humanistic teaching. He has done so without resorting to the heroic image of man found in both classical and nineteenth-century humanism. He has not been driven to exaggerate human goodness or underestimate human malice and bestiality in elucidating man's power to withstand the evils of the world and of his own spirit. What is religiously more significant is that he has left room in his secular philosophy for an equivalent of confession and regeneration. Against the liberal's endless and monotonous trumpet call announcing man's nobility, Camus has made it possible and natural for every man to confess his innate complicity in destruction and death. But against the equally monotonous and more destructive testimony to meaninglessness characteristic of skeptics and nihilists in our day, Camus has encouraged men to believe in compassionate love and to make their lives new by a fresh self-dedication to human service. In the very darkness of our times he has found a way to speak authentically of joy.

Camus' Nobel Prize acceptance speech in 1958 most vividly recapitulates the infernal and spiritual pilgrimage which his own generation has undergone:

> Those men born at the beginning of World War I, who had reached the age of twenty just as Hitler was seizing power and the first revolutionary trials were taking place, who then had to complete their education by facing up to war in Spain, World War II, the regime of concentration camps, a Europe of torture and prisons, must today bring their children and their works to maturity in a world threatened with nuclear destruction. . . . Probably every generation sees itself as charged with remaking the world. Mine, however, knows that it will not remake the world. But its task is perhaps even greater, for it consists in keeping the world from destroying itself. . . .

Starting from nothing but its own negations, (it) has had to
reestablish both within and without itself a little of what constitutes the dignity of life and death.

The age-old rhythm of spiritual death and rebirth sounds,
in a modest way, through Camus' writings. It would be unjust to attribute to him Christian motivations. But in his works
the shape of the Christian witness, however secular and anti-
ecclesiastical its expression, is there. Through crisis and ultimate risk, a man passes to a new affirmation of power and
hope. One discovers hope by acknowledging and experiencing
directly the despair of his time. Hope is not an anesthetic for
despair; the sense of absurdity, futility and suffering continue.
The experience of despair awakens hope as the very necessary
condition for maintaining life. Camus' early concern opening
The Myth of Sisyphus, "There is but one truly serious philosophical problem, and that is suicide," is not absent from his
later works. Increasingly he has found, in the midst of despair,
however, the energy to live; increasingly he has found not
reasons, but power, to say *no* to the drive toward suicide; and
he has transmitted something of that power to the despairing
spirits of many contemporaries. In a strange way he has exalted
the human spirit by enduring its humility, thus giving to an
essential humanism a curiously Christian cast.

Is the endurance of humility Camus' sole resource for ex-
alting the human spirit? Do we see in him a kind of secularized *theologia crucis* devoid of all reference to a doctrine
of creation or created joy? There is evidence that his insights
are more widely extended.

For example, in his Nobel Prize acceptance speech he said,
"I have never been able to forget the sunlight, the delight in
life, the freedom in which I grew up. But although that nos-
talgia explains many of my mistakes and shortcomings, it
doubtless helped me to understand my calling, and it still helps
me to stand implicitly beside all those silent men, who,
throughout the world, endure the life that has been made for
them only because they remember or fleetingly reexperience
free moments of happiness." By speaking thus toward the end

of his life Camus awakens the echo of a kind of religious witness appearing in his earliest works. In *Summer in Algiers* (1936) and *Nuptials* (1938) he recalls the childhood influences of his native Algeria. He dwells especially on the memory of the burning North African sun, the harsh but beautiful landscape, the free and sensuous hours of youthful reveling in the blue Mediterranean. Camus' remembrance of joy, while sensual in character is not orgiastic or merely unrestrained. A melancholy dignity is interwoven into his words as he recognizes the Ephemeral quality of all joys and deliberately turns away from any hope of a peaceful old age or immortality or even of a meaning in death. The flowering of young life carried with it the poignant recognition of transiency and was relished all the more because of this fact. Speaking of his Algerian people, Camus says, "One can find measure [i.e., moderation] as well as excess in the violent and keen face of this race, in this summer sky with nothing tender in it, before which all truths can be uttered and on which no deceptive divinity has traced the signs of hope or redemption. Between this sky and these faces turned toward it, nothing on which to hang a mythology, a literature, an ethic, or a religion, but stones, flesh, stars, and those truths the hand can touch."

While Camus celebrates these ecstatic memories of a human joy bound up with glories of the natural world, he never forgets the melancholy which is native to his forebears and kinsmen and which has been accentuated for him by the humiliations of modern European history. His "invincible summer" at the heart's core is made all the more precious and poignant in relation to the grim realities of personal and social evil. The initial witness of delight is supplemented by the experience of suffering. Conversely the possibility of a redeeming love occurring in the midst of misery is fortified by ineradicable memories of former joy.

In such an astringent conception of suffering curiously touched with ecstasy and fortified by moderation, one feels both the melancholy and naive delight of the ancient Greeks. In their bright and beautiful land, the vision of nature at once nourished their religious sensibilities and reminded them of their transiency and finitude. Nature is both supportive and destructive; it provides the energy of life and sets all limits. Camus' rebellious but creative human spirit derives energy from nature while acknowledging the ultimate triumph of nature over man. It is clear that one religious source of Camus' humanism arises from a Mediterranean, Hellenic, non-biblical view of the chief values of human life. The tendency of the Bible to locate ultimate meaning in history rather than in nature receives a harsh comment from Camus in *The Rebel:* "The profound conflict of this century is perhaps not so much between German ideologies of history and Christian political concepts, which in a certain way are accomplices as between German dreams and Mediterranean traditions—in other words, between history and nature. . . . When nature ceases to be an object of contemplation and admiration, it can be nothing more than material for an action that aims at transforming it."

Camus appears to have found both Hellenic and Christian modes of thought for giving shape to his understanding of man's nature and destiny. He has affirmed in the Greek tradition a kinship between the glory and melancholy of man and the glory and melancholy of nature. He has reproduced the Christian image (without God or Christ) of the descent of the soul into crisis and despair and its resurrection into new strength and meaningfulness. A common religious element in all these affirmations is expressed in the prepositional phrase, "in spite of." He speaks of beauty and ecstasy in spite of transience and terror; of rebellion and truth in spite of confusion of values and ultimate mystery; of freedom and love in spite of human hostility and suffering. His is a religious and theological accomplishment of major proportions. He has challenged sectarian liberalism from beginning to end. Yet, he has advanced beyond its limitations without despising its persistent humanism. The liberal who has become weary of outmoded litanies sung in celebration of the nobility of man, who is also tired of an overly benevolent theism which believes that "all's right with the world," must be attracted into these realms where Camus has lead and where Hellenic and Christian teaching have long dwelt.

The attraction is not unambiguous. Camus remains to some degree an existentialist and his preoccupation with human misery and meaninglessness is not always easy to absorb. The current Christian theology of crisis or the theology of the Cross is even more forbidding to the probing liberal. Nevertheless the probing must be forthcoming, lest liberal religious affirmation simply wither and die of irrelevancy. It is the purpose of these chapters to move into these difficult realms, trusting that the faith of the liberal, though stinging from the abrasion of the Christian and existentialist challenge, may yet be fashioned into a truer substance and more authentic and meaningful form.

4. THE ARENA OF DECISION

The pressure of Christian and existentialist challenges upon religious liberalism represents an opportunity for sympathetic reconstruction and not a call to battle. In conflicts of religious belief, contrary to political and military conflict, one can be "attacked" only by something that secretly dwells within him which he has heretofore ignored or repressed. Seeming intrusions of thought or feeling into one's sensibilities are usually inner discontents clamoring to be released in spite of active prejudices which suppress them. Accordingly, the conflicts among sectarian liberalism and a good deal of the Judeo-Christian tradition and the vigorous insights of modern existentialism represent on a broad cultural scale the unfinished religious questioning which is embodied within every citizen of Western civilization. The individual is the seat of conflicts which have been outwardly crystallized into competing institutions and ideologies. And in the individual first of all lies the arena of ultimate decision.

The religious liberal today must come to terms with at least three major strands which constitute an active and viable religious heritage for him. The first of these three strands is what we have called sectarian liberalism. The religious liberal should not be ashamed of these sectarian influences, even though they have been widely attacked. He will need to preserve something of their optimistic humanism in his religious observance and affirmation. For all its flaws, the appeal of sectarian liberalism is that of an ideal, precious to the whole history of the Western world: the ideal that man's dreams can be fashioned into a progressively more meaningful reality by courageous self-application. Or, as Robert Frost has defined the genius of Europe and America: "The only merit is risking spirit in substantiation." Although the challenges to the substance of sectarian liberal faith point up its limitations and its failure to take into account a more complete range of religious concern, they do not invalidate that faith.

The Judeo-Christian tradition is the second major strand in the liberal's religious heritage. It represents the most tangible, most clearly formed and recognizable center of religious commitment in our culture today. Its validity for the liberal does not lie simply in the historical fact that the ethos of Western civilization, both good and bad, is inconceivable apart from the Judeo-Christian heritage. The Judeo-Christian tradition is also a distinct way of responding to human experience wherein man's life is believed to be blessed by a divine gift. The gift itself is multiform—a state of mind, a way of feeling, a power of action—and from the energy of the gift arises an actual resource for accepting the challenge of the Ideal and struggling for its realization. The power of Judaism and Christianity is not only an abstract "ought" stressing what a man is obligated to do; it is an ever present aid in time of trouble, a spiritual energy and hope in human activity. Also, this heritage is essentially communal, providing a brotherhood of faith and hope more tangible than the sectarian liberal's more abstract community of devotees to the method of free religious inquiry. It is the very definiteness of Judaism and Christianity, in faith, community and action which constitutes both its virtues and its dangers. There is always the possibility of an idolatry of its forms and a consequent loss of the sense of the divine mystery that underlies all religious and cultural formations. There is the possibility of the perversion of its forms to serve alien wills and alien values, perversions which vitiate the faith and institution through essentially irreverent, ignorant or malicious manipulations.

The liberal who accepts with critical awareness the Judeo-Christian heritage and his sectarian liberal heritage should also be sensitive to the third strain of religious substance which lies within his arena of decision—the existentialist. Here the attention is on the imminent, the tangible in contrast to a vaguer focus on abstract ideals or a historical community. He will be fortified in the use of critical intelligence toward everything that is grandiose or corrupting in his religious culture. In this respect, existentialism is a not unlikely partner to the habits of mind proceeding from pragmatism and the scientific method. While preserving the critical realism of these modes of thought, existentialism cuts below them to a more fundamental critique of the human situation. The impact of suffering and futility are honestly acknowledged. The religious person is driven to face with courage the complexity and opacity of his position in the world in relation to the systems of value upon which he depends. Religiously conceived, existentialism encourages a kind heroism of critical judgment, a willingness to believe less than one might wish to believe in order not to believe more than is good or meaningful.

The serious risks of existentialism occur in its tendency to corrode faith in sustaining human institutions or in its stubborn dalliance in cultural and religious emptiness. The excessively critical mind may be a human disguise or substitute for a perverse failure to love either oneself or one's fellow men. It may be not so much a just criticism of inherited customs as a neurotic rejection of the inherited sources of one's well-being. With all its risks existentialism continues to challenge all men, liberal or conservative, who claim to be part of any religious enterprise or community.

The liberal church must, if it is to succeed, be receptive to this threefold challenge and make available to its members aids for coming to personal religious decision. This means not only, or primarily, the provision of classes of study and discussion groups where the issues can be handled in their intellectual formulation. It means that the services of worship in the church, the education and worship of its children, and the programs of community action and service should all reflect as fully and openly as possible this threefold religious substance. Such a church will patronize the arts as an opening toward wider perspectives. Such a church will encourage challengers from outside its own circles of faith to inject their serious concerns. Such a church, above all, will recognize that its members have already been influenced by humanistic, Christian and existentialist forces and will acknowledge that the differing proportion of these ingredients within each person will constitute a varied tapestry of church life and behavior. The liberal church is fated to be somewhat multiform and uncoordinated because of the varieties of people it attracts and because it rightly refuses to promote a uniform constituency by means of creedal tests.

Some liberals may wish to ask, Why stop at three? Why not acknowledge, for instance, the appeal of Eastern mysticism?

If such an appeal is genuinely available, if it has become a truly live option in the experience of particular church members, then the congregation as a whole is well advised to pay attention. However, if the option of oriental faith is introduced as a quasi-romantic stopgap to fill the boredom and emptiness of those who are disenchanted with Western religious conceptions, then there is little promise of meaningful religious growth. A culture, like an individual, is a summation of and transcendence over its own history. If that history is unacknowledged, or if it becomes thoroughly alien, the culture or individual can find no genuine solace in the imposition of exotic substitutes. One's history continues to be efficacious in one's life even when suppressed. All such internal conflicts may be aggravated when a more alien but appealing element is superimposed. There is a wise proverb which asserts, "Blessed is he who remembers his fathers with joy."

The individual's inner dialogue with himself in the arena of personal religious decision is complemented by an overt dialogue throughout the church members. The liberal congregation offers the hope of a larger arena of decision. And within this legitimate function of the church lurk certain illusions deserving of careful examination.

The first of these I would call the illusion of *Olympianism*. Liberals are prone to believe that they occupy the summit of a religious Mount Olympus, that from this height they can give equal and objective attention to everything religious, and that they can put together "their own religion" the way a housewife selects ingredients and cooks a meal. Thus, to speak about synthesizing three or more religious options within liberal religion is to risk a hasty and specious syncretism. Human intelligence is simply not that broad, that sympathetic, nor that adept at synthesizing. In religion, as in culture generally, a person is molded by what particular resources he has been given and by those emphases of temperament and previous decision which have been part of his life. In the words of the poet, Adrienne Rich,

> . . . Our gifts compel,
> Master our ways, and lead us in the end
> Where we are most ourselves.

"Gifts" mean not only what we have been given but, more especially, what we are disposed to give. No such perspective is infinite or truly godlike; and no worship of logic or personal preference can become a divine measuring rod. One may presume to be wholly above the arena of decision and its threefold choices only if one has been genuinely elevated by some additional faith and perspective. Such an elevation is theoretically possible, but seldom actual or relevant for liberal religion as it now exists. One stands within the arena because one's life has been founded there. Decisions will be made not from some imaginary Olympus above the arena, but rather from particular and dominant influences within it.

These warnings against the illusion of Olympianism are simply another way of saying that no man can exercise omniscient discrimination or perfect freedom of judgment. Each person brings to the church his own finite religious offering which helps to complete, but certainly is no substitute for, the whole tapestry of faith and action comprising the religious community.

The concept of the church as a receptacle of diverse contributions brings us to a second illusion which is apt to appear in liberal religion—the illusion of the *Religious Free Market*. Each person is supposed to bring his own religious idiosyncrasies and make them available for free exchange with the contributions of his fellow churchmen. There is a certain appeal to this image. Each liberal is apt to be a fragment of some particular religious background, an ex-Catholic, ex-Jew, or ex-Protestant. He is apt to carry within himself various cultural enthusiasms which are potentially religious: a political affiliation, a passion for certain kinds of education or child-rearing, a devotion to pacifism, or an avocational attachment. It is natural to think of the church as the place where all these separate "goods" are brought together and made available for the benefit of those who have not previously shared them. And certainly the church is the one place in society where such an integrating function can take place, where fragmentary loyalties are given some degree of perspective and order. The ideal relationship between church members is one of complementary differences rather than likenesses, so that one person's emptiness may be satisfied by another's fullness.

Granting some validity to this view of the church, it is important to distinguish the illusion it harbors. Religious convictions are not negotiable like goods offered for exchange. Just as no liberal can claim an Olympian perspective, so he cannot randomly select or transmit articles of faith as a man might win an argument or sell a product. He can at best confess what grips him and he can inquire into its validity and into the relation of his faith to that of another. He cannot assume or discard articles of faith at will. No one is religiously self-constituting, though one should be as religiously self-critical and open-minded as possible.

These limitations do affect the sharing of religious conviction as is demonstrated by the actual behavior of liberal churchmen. It is not easy to accept another's religious substance when it is different from one's own. It is rather more flattering to hear one's own prejudices supported. For all their vaunted freedom and scope of religious concern, liberals are quite capable of settling into a groove of unconscious orthodoxy, enjoying the like-mindedness of people who are all too like-minded and not seizing but avoiding every opportunity to challenge one another on life's most critical issues. It is interest-

ing that liberal churchmen can exhibit a great reticence to con-
front one another with painful ethical or theological issues, lest
any such challenge put too much of a strain on the apparent
harmony of the community. The excuse that is most often
given is that every man should be free to make up his own
mind without undue influence or pressure. Another possible
escape is the belief that theological issues are highly personal
and not debatable.

But because religious convictions are not easily negotiable
is all the more reason for their being shared in open encounter.
In the church at least, your religion is theoretically everyone's
business. The Quakers understand this. Along with their careful preservation of absolute freedom of conscience, they also
are willing to wait upon one another with what they call a
"concern." No subject is taboo, if any man feels he must remon-
strate with his brother. And the brother is obliged to listen
and try to understand the concern of those who are trying to
change his thoughts or his ways. The phrase "loving judgment" is pertinent here. We owe it to one another to make humble and candid appeals for the mutual improvement of our
separate lives and attitudes.

The illusion of liberalism as a Religious Free Market is
therefore twofold: (1) a mistaken pride of religious exchange,
that we actually do share our convictions; (2) a mistaken
reticence toward religious encounter, lest we should reveal our
differences and incite dissension. In countering these illusions,
one needs to be reminded that sureness of personal conviction,
while never transferable, is more meaningful than a tolerant
indecision. And the loving utterance of conviction is usually
more fruitful than silence held in the name of courtesy or
propriety. Martin Buber has said that all life is "meeting," to
which must be added, we meet another in proportion to our
ability to meet and know ourselves.

Such security of religious decision is often difficult for
those who call themselves religious liberals. This in turn gives
rise to a third illusion, that liberal religion is essentially an
Unfulfilled Seeking. Liberals are often excessively afraid of
dogmatism, especially if they are but lately escaped from some

orthodox denomination. They do not like to enter into even a loving controversy over religion. At their backs there still hovers the specter of the Puritan divines who burned women for witchcraft or the present-day bigots who ostracize honest people for unbelief or who vote against a presidential candidate because he has the "wrong" belief. They are so suspicious of many beliefs that they begin to suspect and distrust belief itself. It shows itself in the common attitude that the church is made up not of believers but of seekers after truth. They stress not what a man *has* found but rather that elusive and distant hope of spiritual substance which he is still pursuing.

When one ceases searching, one is spiritually dead. Discoveries in science, art or religion should stimulate further search, not discourage it. But it is foolish to deny that nothing has ever been found—and not only foolish, but pathological. It may be that many of the liberals are so empty spiritually that they envy one who is full and, in the name of continued unfulfilled search, they unconsciously disparage his fullness and thus comfort themselves for their own spiritual failures. In one of Dorothy Sayers' books on Dante, she makes this point with devastating candor, saying, "Despite all our surface liking for toughness and violence, ours is a timid generation, wincing at decision and envious of other men's conclusions." The painter, Pablo Picasso, who could scarcely be accused of religious dogmatism, also sees through the idolatry of searching when it is put in opposition to finding. He writes: "In my opinion, to search means nothing in painting. To find, is the thing. The one who finds something, no matter what it might be, at least arouses our curiosity, if not our imagination. When I paint my object is to show what I have found and not what I am looking for."

Not everyone strikes gold, but a good vein of copper may be a useful discovery. Unless a man knows what he has found to date, unless he can appreciate some value in it while realizing its limitations, unless he can risk his findings in open encounter, he is not yet born spiritually. Pure search is pure emptiness. To *find* in the religious sense is to be aware of a fullness of reality beyond one's power of total assimilation and yet not beyond one's power to choose and be committed. Contrary to the bias of sectarian liberalism, it must be urged that mankind has experienced religion primarily as a gift and a finding, a present corporate reality laying hold of its people and attracting their consent. Once the gift has been communally acknowledged, a people is then released to appropriate, develop and freely interpret what has been given. Cultural achievement arises out of the gift but does not provide its substance.

If the foregoing analysis is correct, we may now clarify the arena of religious decision in which the liberal stands. It is not enough to take note of sectarian liberalism, Christianity and existentialism (the three contemporary religious claims which are paramount in Western culture). It is also important to see these areas of religious meaning in their historical depth, that we may better understand whence we have come and where we are.

Two of these strands in our contemporary arena derive in part from a common origin. Both the confident humanism of the sectarian liberal and the existentialists' wrestle with death and despair are rooted in the experience and insights of ancient Greek culture. The Greeks knew how to rejoice and how to exercise their abundant human powers. Yet, their joyous affirmations and cultural greatness were produced against the background of a sense of tragedy. The task of reconstructing liberal religion is therefore in part a rediscovery of the several dimensions of the Greek mind and spirit.

An even more influential discovery lies in the biblical mind and spirit. Here we may find (1) an indirect humanism standing in support of sectarian liberal concerns; (2) a powerful existentialism illuminating man's perennial subjection to the threat of despair; (3) a communal affirmation of faith and hope in and beyond the reality of tragedy. The presence of these several religious strands in biblical literature is by no means harmonious at all points. The religious gifts of the Bible are sharp-edged and not to be easily assimilated *in toto*. The recovery of the biblical heritage in an atmosphere of free inquiry is a complicated and fascinating task and requires a new maturity on the part of liberals. They must lay aside their emotional antagonisms to biblical language and thought and plunge resolutely into the Bible's diverse symbolism and subtle insight.

Every introspective man today who is also sensitive to the condition of his fellow human beings has something both of Greece and Israel within him. The manner in which he conducts his life may resemble the more ancient forms little or not at all, but these two ancient cultures serve to dramatize the ingredients of his own nature. The proportionate influence of each culture will vary among individuals. Just as every person must find some resolution of these tensions within himself, so the church is the larger arena where the inward struggle is recognized outwardly; it is the place where men of good will are making a common and public effort toward harmonizing the conflicting elements among themselves, even as the contrasting strings of a musical instrument may be tuned to different, but harmonious tones. The church seeks to provide the social setting and support for the otherwise lonely and often impossible religious task facing the individual.

5. THE MELANCHOLY AND RATIONALISM OF THE GREEKS

Hellenic civilization has given to the world certain religious and philosophical prototypes which have influenced both modern existentialism and sectarian liberalism. It is well to identify these prototypes precisely and to note the tensions among them, which appeared in ancient Greece and which reappear today dividing the existentialist from the liberal.

Among the ancient Greeks a proto-existentialism appears to be considerably older than the development of their classic rationalism. Their earliest myths and rituals are at once sacred celebrations of the natural beauty and vitality of the world and a melancholy recognition of the ultimate pathos and hopelessness at the base of all human life. We have seen the same dichotomy in the works of Albert Camus. The glory of the world implants its "invincible summer" in the human heart; but an unavoidable pathos requires that man must learn to live courageously without any transcendent hope as he moves between the two mysteries of birth and death.

In contrast to biblical religion, Greek thought and feeling is oriented to nature rather than history. The oldest indications of Greek religion appear to attribute man's origin and welfare to earthly powers, to the growth of the grains and the fruits following the rhythm of the seasons. These early myths and rituals describe man as earth-born, as having his origin not in animal procreation but in vegetable generation from the ground. The aboriginal Thebans were thought to have grown as grain from the planting of the divine Cadmus. The myth of Jason, wherein an army is sprouted from the dragon's teeth, reflects the same ancient theme. Many local cults celebrated the belief that the Greeks had originated in their own land and were not immigrants from some other place. And this origin was thought to be agricultural and spontaneous rather than by sexual generation.

The Greek belief in a sacred earth-origin is not at all similar in spirit to what is called "materialism" today. The primordial materials were thought to be alive and divine. The later problem of the separation of mind and matter, of spirit and its material substratum had not yet arisen. A sense of the sacredness of nature pervaded Greek sensibilities. The Earth Mother, under many names or local manifestations, is the source of the spring growth and the summer harvest. She recedes in vital powers with the dying year and is reborn again in the spring. Her own transformations from Koré (Maiden) to Kourotrophos (Bearer of Young) dramatize the Greeks' central devotion to the powers of fertility in the early stages of their religion.

Later, perhaps as a consequence of the invasion of northern tribes beginning about 1300 B.C., the emphasis on fertility was transformed into a more political and juridical image. The introduction of the Olympian pantheon followed, and with it arose the image of Zeus, not as a creator, but as a warrior and supreme ruler among the contending generations of the gods. But even then, the orientation to nature was not destroyed; it was simply made more manifold and complicated. The aboriginal religious culture of Greece, oriented to agriculture, was supplanted by the military ethos and mythology of the northern invaders. Through these developments appeared myths of the origin of the world in terms of the sexual generation of the gods.

Hesiod's *Theogany* preserves this mythology in literary form. To the primordial deities he attributes great size, formlessness, and a darkness similar to the original Chaos (Abyss or Empty Space) from which all things come. Erebus and Tartarus (Dark Space) are the parents of the powers of the Day and the Sky. These original natural phenomena were also conceived of as living deities. The primitive earth (Gaia) produces spontaneously the vault of the heavens with its fixed stars

(Ouranos). Then Gaia unites with her son, Ouranos, and the various features of the earth come into being. Some are beautiful and some hideous. Mountains, forests, the seas and rivers appear along with vast destructive monsters such as the hundred-headed Hydra or the one-eyed Cyclopes.

In these births of the gods according to Hesiod, the original spontaneous generation gives way to the method of sexual procreation. Sexual generation is often given a pre-animalistic reality, as when the Heavens were thought to impregnate the Earth by means of rain. Thus man's procreative powers were related to a primordial natural process. This theme is suggested in Hesiod's contention that Eros, Love, is one of the very oldest gods. Either by the fertility of the Earth or by the primordial attraction of male and female, the multifaceted world comes into being. Creation is fertility and procreation. The profusion of Greek myths describing later gods as offsprings of earlier gods, describing also the generations of mankind as earth-born or as descended from heroes who were originally offsprings of gods, attests to the truly vitalistic quality of the Greek spirit. As this people looked out on the sunlit brilliance of their fertile, temperate land and fish-crowded seas, they celebrated the profusion and confusion of superabundance and attributed to the fecundity of the world an essentially sacred character.

Even as the Greeks celebrated the joyous abundance of nature, they also confessed to its deadly conflicts. They saw in it the inevitable source of their own pathos. Hesiod viewed the emergence of the natural world as an uncertain race between the fertility of the mothers and the destructiveness of the fathers. Ouranos became disgusted with his heterogeneous progeny and proceeded to confine them all in Tartarus, the great gulf of darkness below the earth. The beautiful Titans, sons and daughters of Ouranos representing the benign powers of earth, were indiscriminately exiled with their siblings, the loathsome monsters. The wholesale negation of being caused an unredeemable conflict between the primordial parents, Ouranos and Gaia, since the mother grieved for her own and would not consent to their deathlike exile. She begged her children to revolt and found them all fearful except Kronos, the youngest and wiliest. It was he who, having been given an adamantine sickle by his mother, castrated his father, Ouranos, and threw him into Tartarus while freeing the generation of his brothers and sisters.

Kronos (the Latin name, Saturn) later swallowed his own offspring because his father had prophesied that he too would be overthrown by a similar revolt of the next generation. This prophecy relates to a brilliant and paradoxical touch in Hesiod's narrative. The blood of Ouranos' emasculation gave birth to the Furies and to Aphrodite. The former were god-desses of vengeance, who tend to multiply the crimes of the fathers among the sons, and the latter, the Goddess of Love who eternally brings forth new life. Time is a race between life and death, a hunger to produce and an insatiable urge to destroy. So Hesiod tells how Zeus, offspring of Kronos, saved from being swallowed through the connivance of his mother, caused his brothers and sisters, the Gods and Goddesses, to be disgorged and led them in successful revolt against Kronos and the Titans. Not all the Titans fought the Gods. Some like Prometheus (whom Plato interprets as "Forethought'), Themis (Order and Justice), Mnemosyne (Memory, also Mother of the Muses), and Eurynome (Beauty) joined to support Zeus. From them were born the Hours, Muses, and Charities—all the deities of measure and harmony. Zeus himself sought to estab-lish a sovereign order over all.

After the victory of Zeus over the Titans, the pattern of heavenly rule which emerges is of great significance. Zeus himself is not primarily a creator, although he has his share of offspring. Both the humane and the vital powers are seen to derive from the earlier generation, to derive from a more pri-mordial origin and depth. These powers, by the arrogance of fathers and the jealousy and connivance of mothers, are in conflict. Wife rebels against husband, son rises up against father. Fertility is in conflict with tyranny. Zeus's supreme power is political. As orderer, as one who holds the conflicting powers of nature in precarious balance, he is unrivaled. But he cannot command these powers himself and must grant to them some sphere of autonomous activity. The continuing warfare of the older and later deities was thought by the Greeks to be the underlying cause of the conflicts among men. So the wanderings of Odysseus arose in part out of the enmity between Athena and Poseidon; and the final triumph of Athena in this regard sprang from her superior political influence over Zeus.

Many of the themes we noted in Camus' thought are thus anticipated in the Greek mythology. The primordial powers are inscrutable and only partially controllable. They represent beauty and fertility as well as destruction and death in nature. By rational control, courageous warfare, and judicious management, the peculiarly human powers can, for a brief while, enjoy the goodness of the earth. But the sickness of conflict and murder is also within man and death is his final end. This is not to negate the importance of rational order, but rather to make it all the more desirable, since only in moderation and in the balancing of life against its violent extremes is there even a temporary glimmer of hope for man. Only if the savagery in nature and in man is held in check can he enjoy for a season nature's power and loveliness. Such is Greek courage arising out of their sorrow of the world.

It is accurate, I believe, to speak of the melancholy of the Greeks as sorrow of the world. The word "sorrow" carries with it overtones of poignancy and regret, a sense of the goodness that has been, that might yet be, that is tragically lost. One cannot read the *Odyssey* without being struck by the frequency of Odysseus' tears—not tears of remorse, but tears of regret. He weeps for the death of his young men, for his forced departure from so many places of joyous adventure, and for the spoliation of his lands and household. As a great adventurer, he is the prototype of the courageous Western man launching out from the safe mooring into the unknown. Deeply immersed in life, he loves the fragile beauty of the world and its materials and enjoys the loving loyalty of his companions. By exercising superior wit he hears the deadly Sirens' songs and threads between Scylla and Charybdis without being destroyed. By adroit prayers and sacrifice he gains favor from the gods who are well disposed and avoids punishment from those gods who are hostile. No hedonist ever relished the joys of love, food, song, sport, navigation, even warfare more than Odysseus. Yet it is entirely consistent and accurate for Homer to have Menelaus say of Odysseus: "No man of the Achaeans deserved so greatly or labored as greatly as great Odysseus labored and endured. For him it was written that the outcome should be but sorrow upon sorrow." (Book IV.) This is not indiscriminate sorrow; it is sorrow of *the world*. It is a realization of man's inability to maintain indefinitely his privileged position. The powers that surround him are too great. Sooner or later, in the counsels of the gods or in the darker designs of the fates, some evil will strike through the thin shield by which mortal man seeks to protect himself.

There is no recourse in the *Odyssey* to a suprahuman justice. Father Zeus must, at Athena's bidding, allow her to outwit the hostility of his brother Poseidon toward the wandering Odysseus. Or as Athena says to Zeus in Book I: "But come, let us put our heads together to contrive the man's return; then will Poseidon have to swallow his bile. Against the concert of the immortals he cannot stand alone." Zeus cannot act as Jehovah and flatly decree the outcome. He must enter into a plot. Such a view of life simply continues the ancient mythological theme that creation is an unstable mixture of many Powers, continually engaged "in dubious battle." There are degrees of strength among them, but no Absolute Strength. The gods shower a confusing alternation of support and hostility on man, making his fate the function of no single power. The control of destiny is temporarily in man's own hand. This proto-existentialist note is whispered in the Greek epics, not announced boldly lest the Gods be jealous. When Odysseus is shipwrecked and is seeking to swim ashore to the Phaeacians' land (Book V), he despairs lest Zeus has abandoned him to death. Seeing a river's mouth near at hand, he prays to the River God and is suddenly swept from the fierce seas into a calm estuary where he can swim ashore. The religious essence involved here is not that of the unfailing piety of the Jew toward the inscrutable benevolence of Jehovah; it is rather, a human alertness to address the right prayer at the right time to the right deity. In modern terms, this is to say that man depends upon the powers of nature and must also maintain himself in spite of nature's hostility and indifference to his needs. What tips the scale between life and death and grants temporary extension of life is *man's* ability to lay hold of the right power at the right time. Nature as a whole is not "personally" concerned either to slay or save. Nature is a variety of drives within which man must live as best he can. And even as man loves the beauty of the world and relishes its particular joys, he must also know the sorrow of the world by which his life is finally undone.

The Greek view of this human situation is complicated by the conflicting natural drives that dwell *within* man as well as beyond him. His "hubris" is his vitality; it is also the occasion of his downfall. A kind of justice operates in the world of Greek tragedy which is oriented not so much to give the good man his due as it is to inflict on the evil man his punishment. The evil can be done unwittingly (Oedipus), or out of a sense of personal pride and honor (Agamemnon at Aulis), or out of a fierce and compelling love for revenge (Clytemnestra and Electra), or out of near madness and derangement (Medea). In all these cases the moral issue is less paramount than the judicial issue, the balance of power. Offend what is powerful and it will retaliate without regard to right and wrong. A curse will be transmitted from father to son, as in the *Oresteia,* just as the curse of warfare and murder was transmitted from one generation of gods to the next as described in Hesiod's *Theogany.* Man can envisage justice and misery because man *is man.* But man-in-nature comes to tragic ends in spite of his concern for the good.

More acutely than any of the other Greek myths, the story of Prometheus bears witness to man's fundamental and uncomforted estrangement. The Titan, Prometheus, who dares by stealth to help men become more nearly like the gods, is subjected by Zeus to fearful punishment and torture. Arising from the pre-Zeus generation of creator-gods, Prometheus represents the best type of man, using and controlling the benevolent powers of nature while shielding himself and others from her cruelties. Such poise threatens the superiority of Zeus's untroubled Olympian existence. Although Zeus does not even have the power to recover the stolen gifts of civilization from man, he can out of spite make Prometheus miserable and, by the ruse of Pandora's Box, send upon man a host of pestilential woes. Thus the myth suggests that man has a case against the universe and that men should boldly try to outwit hardship, fate and even the gods themselves whenever possible. To have a case against the universe is to experience a sorrow of the world and to endure, in the midst of courage and adventure, a thoroughgoing melancholy. It is to entertain a secret scorn toward divine agency as Prometheus does, or an open, defiant scorn as do the warring sons of Oedipus and his cynical uncle, Creon.

Somewhere in between ecstasy and despair is a poise born of intelligence and flavored with deep melancholy, a poise which has the power if only temporarily to sustain life in all its hazards. Such poise, which Odysseus concretely exemplified and Aristotle celebrated more abstractly in his "golden mean" and his "great-souled man," and which has been nurtured in stoic philosophy and rejuvenated by the probings of existentialism, has come down to our day as an ideal for man. Gilbert Murray could have been speaking for Albert Camus when, in describing the essence of high Hellenic religious culture, he said: "Just for a few great generations, it would seem, humanity rose to a sufficient height of self-criticism and self-restraint to reject these dreams of self-abasement or megalomania." [1] Man is not god, but neither should man be abased in slavery to any god, especially to a god literally conceived and manipulated by some other man. Murray attributes this achievement to a reform movement in the Olympian religion undertaken by the Athenians under the civilizing aegis of their patron goddess, Athena. He also confesses that the whole process ended in failure. The tendency to deify the king came back into state religion as the people again committed the sins of megalomania and consequent self-abasement.

[1] Gilbert Murray, *Five Stages of Greek Religion*, Beacon Press, 3d. ed., 1951.

It is not too much of an oversimplification to say that Greek humanism is rooted in the divided and tension-filled character of Greek theism. Having no single and absolute divine authority which could be trusted to propagate man's ultimate well-being, the philosophies of the Greeks were forced to recognize the large role of human decision in the course of human history. Man himself must steer his course amid the profusion of external powers which surround him.

The emphasis on man led to a certain parting of the ways in the development of Greek civilization. If, as in the case of Odysseus, man's primary powers are seen to be a defiant courage and vitality with intellect and wit devoted to practical affairs rather than to understanding, the resulting picture of human life is partly similar to the existentialism of Albert Camus. But if, as in the model of Aristotle's "Great-Souled Man," the element of rational understanding and control are emphasized, we see a prototypical essentialism akin to modern liberalism. The key to the difference between these two strains within Greek thought is their differing conceptions of the sources of human decision.

If one's decisions are based on "Themis"—the proper way to propitiate angry deities and not anger beneficent ones— reasoning itself is a combination of custom and native canniness, an instinct for moderation in threading one's way among life's unknowable influences. But if Reason is viewed in the honored station to which Plato and Aristotle assigned it, as capable of penetrating to Being Itself, and discovering the Essence of all things, then man takes on a godlike and ultimately secure status above the usual tides of human affairs by the mere exercise of his rational powers. Plato represents Socrates as believing that his life of Reason had prepared him for a blessed immortality. Aristotle was bold enough to suggest that the fulfillment of "Theoretical Reason" put man into direct relationship with the reasonableness of Being itself, a reasonableness which he called "Thinking about Thinking," and which he attributed to God and man as a common power.

This powerful drive in Greek culture toward rational transcendence over the accidents of fate and fortune reached its climax in Plato and Aristotle and subtly wrought a major change in basic conceptions of reality. Under the triumph of classical Hellenic rationalism, the universe came to be regarded as essentially knowable and rationally ordered. The old fear of spirits and fate, of the uncontrollable and inscrutable, gave way to what was considered an enlightened conception of reality and of human existence. What we have called a proto-existentialist vitalism and melancholy turned, through the strength of Greek rationalistic humanism, into a proto-essentialism.

The sectarian liberal spirit today is a beneficiary of the rationalist strand in this ancient parting of the ways. Liberals have depended heavily upon assumptions which the Greeks in the age of Plato and Aristotle originally propounded. The liberal's assurance that the natural world is essentially amenable to human understanding and control is related to the Greek assurance that the world is constituted so that its very essence can be understood. One is reminded of Plato's belief that Being and Good are one, that the eternally static center of reality is accessible to man and can fortify man's well-being when he is in direct contact with it. Man's rational faculty is the bridge to the serenity of Being. By letting this faculty rule his life, man is saved from the tragedies of helpless involvement in the world of appearances, of flux, and Becoming. While liberalism may have largely lost the ecstatic and mystical dimension in Plato's rationalism, it holds to one of its major derivatives: the Aristotelian faith in the essential reasonableness of experience and of the concrete processes which regulate the tangible world. Modern science generally shares this assumption. A liberal scientific outlook has the serenity of Hellenic rationalism without its transcendent reference. It attributes an orderliness to the realm of Becoming which Plato found only in Being.

Thus the particular substance and content of modern rationalism has moved away from its classic formulations in Greek culture. But the form and spirit of modern rationalism is not greatly different. Whatever are the mysteries of reality, man's power to cope with them is innate and is manifested largely through the exercise of his reason. The answers to the most serious questions about the meaning of human existence are given in terms of self-discipline, personal choice and control of the will, all of which are under the guidance of the rational faculties. Existence will always have its obdurate areas and its unmanageable powers. The best that man can hope for is to make rational probes towards the essences of existence. And while the sciences are quite different in method and content from what they were in the time of Aristotle, the spirit of rational inquiry for the sake of human well-being is unchanged. "Salvation" was understood humanistically by Aristotle as it is by liberals today. The three principles of sectarian liberalism which were discussed in Chapter 1 owe their origin mainly to classical Greek rationalism: (1) man must achieve his own religious orientation and behavior; (2) man has the innate powers to do so; (3) free men deciding and acting in their own freedom will find a natural social harmony among one another.

It is worthy of note that liberals in the last century, like the rationalists in classical Greece, have tended to disregard the appeal of non-essentialist philosophies in their own time. Just as the followers of Plato could not listen to Heraclitus, so the modern liberal does not listen to Kierkegaard or Nietzsche. There is pride of accomplishment in rationalist thinking which tends to be condescending toward religious piety or philosophical despair. As Gilbert Murray has shown, the essential nature of original Greek piety was a respect and awe of the gods, without claim to understanding their nature and without hope of rivaling their felicity. Classic Greek rationalism tended to move away from such modesty and to raise the pretense of understanding the very essence of being. The boldness, power, and scope of Platonic and Aristotelian philosophy left a nearly indelible mark on the Western mind which, in the spirit of true Greek moderation, the existentialists have been trying to erase. In speaking of Dostoevski's "Underground Man" William Barrett observes, "What Dostoievski is saying, through his tormented and oppressed little hero, is that human life must be more than pure reason, and to attempt to reduce it to the latter is to destroy it, even if we make that reduction in the name of universal enlightenment." In a subtle way Greek rationalism moved into the very megalomania which Greek piety had always feared. One is reminded of Paul Tillich's dictum that all knowledge is a combination of union and detachment. When the element of detachment becomes dominant (in order that the knower might manipulate and control the known), the knower becomes estranged from reality; and that which is known, even though it is a human being, is reduced to the status of an object without life, subjectivity, or values of its own. The knower and known are each dehumanized by being subjected, voluntarily or not, to an abstract system in which there is no room for individual freedom or for the loving union of separate beings.

In our own day Albert Camus has applied the Hellenic virtue of moderation to the equally Hellenic temptation toward an oppressive rationalism or a dogmatic scientism. A teaching of Pascal is reflected in these concerns. The French mathematician-philosopher maintained that in order to achieve a moderate position one must not submit either to despair and nihilism or to the pretensions of any absolutism. The former leads to the claim of bestiality, the latter to the claim of an angelic life. The nihilist subtly absolutizes his own private decisions and claims for himself a world without due recognition of his neighbor. The absolutist anxiously pursues control over the variables and imponderables of his life. He does not recognize that the very sorrow of the world is also his sorrow, its woes and fallibilities are his also, and every strenuous effort to be transcendent over such ambiguities only plunges him deeper into them. Camus' existentialism, like its Greek prototypes, accepts the ambiguities of life without hope of total victory over them and without despair of significant action in relation to them. A man may thus continue to love the world that will finally destroy him; he will acknowledge a dependence on the world without yielding his right and duty of free decision; he will live purposively but without hope, in a precarious poise between skepticism and dogma, between cynicism and pride.

Such a sober yet well-founded philosophy has peculiar

appeal. This is especially true today when, as Camus suggests, our task is not much that of remaking the world but rather of saving it from the compulsive self-destruction of fanaticism or boredom. A "strange love" survives best when founded on a realistic melancholy which will not be seduced by false hopes and become an instrument of hate and destruction. It sometimes seems, in the gray and threatening light of our era, as though only this much of faith remains to soothe the pain and despair of modern man. Accordingly, one wonders why liberals in greater number have not made the transition toward an existentialist orientation under the pressure of modern events and patterns of thought.

Perhaps such a transition is even now underway. But it is safe to prophesy that no large scale shift will take place, at least not swiftly. The reason is that there is buried in the liberal's collective religious history a certain non-Hellenic resource which tends to sustain his optimism in spite of the exposed and weakened position of modern rationalism. This support is rooted in the background of Jewish covenant theology. To that background let us now turn.

6. THE COVENANT OF ISRAEL

For all the similarities between Greek and Hebraic culture, there is one significant difference between them. For the ancient Greeks, man's relationship to the natural world was thought to be basically insecure; for the ancient Jews it was considered basically secure. What we have called the proto-existentialism of the Greeks was filled with the pathos of human existence, the sense of the ultimate hazard of life, of the brevity, ambiguity and temporary nature of human happiness, and finally with the feeling of the utter meaninglessness of death. Even the philosophical rationalism of the Greeks could not eliminate this distrust of experienced phenomena. The triumph of reason was achieved by transcending the ordinary condition of man and, in Plato's case, by anticipating personal immortality.

Jewish culture harbored no such battle instinct toward the phenomenal world and the immediate features of human experience. The religious achievement of Judaism was to introduce an attitude of loving relationship between man and his environment and developing history. The trust which the Greek rationalists had vested in the rationality of essences (in contrast to sensory appearances) was extended by the Jews into the phenomena of everyday experience. "The earth is the Lord's," and therefore it is good. The Jews were not troubled by the sense of cleavage between spirit and matter such as we find in Greek rationalism. Their one God was believed to be present in the course of history, never isolated in a transcenden-

tal realm. This Jewish legacy more than anything else prevents
the rationalism of liberals from reverting to a more melancholy,
more nearly existentialist, point of view. Stated more precisely,
my thesis is that liberals have taken into themselves a secularized version of Jewish covenant theology.

The Jews' faith in their divinely given covenant presupposes a decidedly non-Greek conception of creation. The
imagery of the first chapter of Genesis connotes a creative
power that is single and unopposed, possessed of infinite wisdom, and expressive of an unlimited love pouring forth the
abundance of created things for the sheer delight of creating.
The refrain, "God saw that it was good," with its climax,
"And God saw everything that he had made, and behold, it
was very good," speaks of a cosmic delight in the details of
the world and of a primordial harmony among all things
moving within the circle of the Creator's love. The first negative note comes only when man willfully departs from the
harmonious paradise over which he had been given dominion.
Until that fateful defection all things directly reflect the
perfect love of God. But even with the myth of the fall, there
is no cancellation of the original provision in the creation myth
that man shall have dominion over the earth, that he shall subdue and replenish all existence, and that he shall have the
power to name all things which, liberally interpreted, means
the power to discern an intellectual order in all reality. Subsequent Jewish commentary on the first chapter of Genesis
has produced this lovely meditation:

> Some sages claim that all the creatures of the earth, the seas
> and the sky, were created before the First Man, so that he should
> never, in his pride, claim that he was God's favorite and was
> created before the others, even though he was given dominion
> over all the other creatures right from the beginning. Others
> claim that the world was created to the last blade of grass in
> preparation for Man, as one prepares for a distinguished and
> beloved guest.[1]

[1] Joseph Gaer, *The Lore of the Old Testament*, Little, Brown and Company, 1951,
p. 35.

Our modern skepticism toward the literal interpretation of all mythology need not destroy for us the force of mythical symbolism in expressing fundamental attitudes toward the world as a human environment. How different is this Jewish sense of the inner sacredness and ultimate harmony of all things, from the Greek myths' conception of the primordial origins steeped in conflict and in bloodshed as well as love! To the Greek, the elements of hostility and consequent destruction are primordial in the nature of all things, first in the warfare of the generations of the gods and then in mankind's own struggle for existence. In the mythical picture of the struggle between Prometheus, symbol of a divine humanity, and Zeus, King of the Gods, man's well-being is achieved in spite of the hostility of the mightiest of divine powers and at the cost of a terrible and undeserved suffering. Prometheus' only consolation is his pride in his superior wisdom and in his ultimate freedom from the will of Zeus. He responds to the supernatural powers with godlike scorn. His compassion is toward the human creatures of his own fashioning. Zeus is neither man's creator nor his sustainer, but rather man's jealous and punishing tyrant. In sharp contrast, the biblical creation myth announces an original goodness in all things great and small, implies that a divine will is working behind the progression of a benign history. Man, in the image of God, is seen as kind of a cocreator and coruler of the world under God's ultimate lordship. Destiny is envisaged as hopeful.

The myth of Adam and Eve takes place against this background of the good-that-might-have-been. Man in his pride seeks to become like God, because of all creation man *is* the most nearly godlike and consequently is tempted to be subject to none but himself. This ultimate self-inflation is symbolized by Adam's disobedience. Therefore, God must recognize a degree of hostility between man and the world as a consequence of man's will toward self-estrangement. The "punishment" for man's prideful disobedience is not a fundamental enmity between God and man or between man and nature. It is rather the abandonment of man to the ambiguities of his own finite intelligence and powers. Man's hypocrisy in thinking that his powers were or could be infinite is thus justly rewarded. The myth attests symbolically to a conflict of harmony *and* estrangement in man and to an unending restlessness toward the recovery of a lost peace and inner security.

Again the Jewish theological instincts differ sharply from the Greek. The Jews did not regard the estrangement of man as ultimate and final, as though God were glad to put man permanently into an inferior and suffering state. Instead, God is conceived as taking the initiative to recover a right relationship between himself and his human creatures. Out of this far-reaching intuition the Jews evolved their covenant theology.

The initiative of God toward man's salvation appears in least expected situations, against seemingly insurmountable odds. Abraham is surprised by the three Angelic Visitors and by their promise that his aging and childless wife, Sarah, shall bear him a son (Gen. 18). Jacob, a refugee from his murderous brother, Esau, is granted a vision of a divine destiny while in lonely exile in the wilderness. And Joseph, the enslaved exile in a foreign land, becomes the unlikely instrument for the divine rescue of his people and their birth as a nation under Moses. These, and many other instances, illustrate the vivid Jewish sense of the victory of God and his people over every estrangement in the most unlikely and seemingly hopeless situations.

This essentially religious optimism had its obligations for man. These obligations were spelled out in various formulations of the covenant between God and his people. The Jew believed himself to be chosen not for automatic felicity but primarily for the gift of a set of commandments. The initial and crucial part of what God gives to men in their condition of self-estrangement is a new law of righteousness which they must obey of their own free will. With obedience comes the response of divine rescue and sustenance. Without obedience, the conditions of estrangement worsen. The burden of the covenant is that it leaves its violators more miserable than if they had never accepted it.

In primitive Greek thought there is no such clear avenue of rescue from human conflict and woe as the Jews intuited.

The favor of certain gods toward individuals was quite apart from any standard of moral behavior and was expressive, rather, of the arbitrary alignments of conflicting power characteristic of nature generally. It may be argued that there is a similarly arbitrary note in the biblical tales. Especially in the J and E documents of the Old Testament, Jehovah arbitrarily favors the Jews and arbitrarily punishes their enemies. There is no denying the primitive nationalism inherent in these sources. But the significant difference from their Greek counterparts is that God's favor is always in covenantal relationship to man's righteousness. It is a favor for which man must make payment in obedience. And obedience is for the sake of a way of life destined to bring eventual felicity to all men, not to the Jews alone.

Thus there is an austerity and realism to Jewish historical optimism. Human well-being is man's responsibility as well as God's gift. The covenant poses for man an immense obligation to fulfill his ethical responsibility and to endure with patience all the delays and frustrations common to the dedicated life. For instance, when the patriarch, Jacob, was called to return home and face the danger of his hostile brother, Esau, he had to wrestle all night with an emissary of the Lord and was permanently lamed in the encounter. The symbolism of this tale suggests that one's election to a divine destiny is also a crippling of the body and a constant threat to one's well-being.

These dangers imbue the optimism of the Jews with a certain dogged and persistent quality; it is an optimism won and preserved in spite of immense difficulties and ordeals. These attributes are symbolized in Jacob's refusal to release his Angelic Antagonist as they wrestle by the Jabbok River (Gen. 32). Having entered the covenant, he would not forfeit it, but said, "I will not let you go unless you bless me." The merely human antagonist in the encounter will insist that blessing should accompany the high and lonely journey of obedience to God. Jacob's insistence prevailed and he was given, along with his blessing, a new name: "Israel: He who strives with God."

Jewish piety has undergone a very subtle development.

On the one hand, it has acknowledged the utter sovereignty of the Almighty and has accepted with patience every outrageous and irrational turn of events as the consequence of God's mysterious will. On the other hand, Israel has striven with God. It has sought to probe the veil of mystery, to understand the causes behind events and how to influence them favorably for man. This twofold emphasis is present in the well-known Kaddish prayer of the eighteenth-century Rabbi, Levi Isaac of Berditshev. Having said, "Good morning to you, Lord of the World," he goes on to press "a legal matter" by saying that God's many heavy demands on the people of Israel are given in a world where other nations are much greater and more powerful than Israel. The implication is clear that Israel has not been properly compensated for her woes and the Rabbi is protesting. The Rabbi then utters the traditional opening line of the Kaddish, "Glorified and sanctified be His great name," and continues, "I shall not go hence nor budge from my place until there be a finish, until there be an end of exile." [2] Like Jacob, the pious Rabbi honors the Lord, but he will not let him forget his promises of blessing to the people of Israel. It could be said that not only Jewish piety but also Jewish persistence in hope have been responsible for the remarkable longevity and creativity of this people. There is an indestructible trust, despite their history of hardship and disillusionment, in the ultimate correlation and harmony between human righteousness and the march of natural and historical events.

In these several ways the Jews have achieved a significantly different sense of harmony with the world from that of Greek rationalism. The transcendence over suffering and estrangement envisaged in Plato and Aristotle was primarily intellectual and aesthetic. It disregarded the distractions of ordinary history and sought to express a realm above the experiential and historical. The Jew's harmony with the Creator and with creation was established on a moral basis and was believed to occur as the fruit of obedience and faithfulness throughout every ordeal in life.

This contrast in attitude may be translated into secular

[2] *In Time and Eternity,* ed. by N. H. Glatzer, Schocken Books, 1946, p. 94.

terms. The Greeks suggested that there is in man's mind a resource for ultimate serenity and harmony through wisdom. The Jews suggested that a serene and harmonious life occurs in the degree to which one gives himself to a loving care and support of his fellow men. There is no absolute cleavage here; Greek wisdom implies the right ordering of society, and Jewish righteousness implies not only the enlightenment of divine revelation but also the application of human intelligence. But whereas the Greek tended to emphasize the possibility of man's individual salvation through wisdom, the Jew stressed the *obligation* of man's social salvation through justice and love. Men in community must make the sacrificial effort and the world is such as to provide a meaningful setting and response.

Sectarian liberalism profits by its biblical antecedents. To the Greek passion for rational clarity and the Greek faith that reality is amenable to rational investigation is added the Jewish belief in the meaningfulness of the pursuit of righteousness in the world. The liberal is ultimately hopeful of the future even though he may not express his hope in biblical or theological terms. He believes that man and nature are constituted for cooperative endeavor and mutual support. Not that nature is partial to human values as such, but rather that nature is malleable. Human effort can make her yield benefits and blessings. The liberal's world has an ultimate dependability about it, a responsiveness to the intelligence and the mutual good will of man. Nature will never betray men who live together in righteousness, but will bless them. Not only is man capable of fulfilling the good life but he is also under obligation to do so. His dignity as a man is also a noble burden, and thus can be a source of great pain as well as joy. His obligation to subdue and replenish the earth carries with it the threat that if he only subdues and does not replenish, if he rules without fulfilling the obligations of nurturing love, he has broken the "covenant" of man and nature and renders himself liable to retribution.

The secularized version of any theological teaching usually involves some definite alterations in the teaching itself. The sectarian liberal's translation of covenant theology is certainly not a literal translation. The very removal of the divine dimension forces definite changes. In the Jewish heritage, man's obligation and hope are believed to be derived directly from the Creator. The modern liberal is considerably less certain that there are any objective standards available to man. In the Jewish heritage of covenant theology, human suffering is rather readily interpreted as consequent upon man's failure, whether conscious or unconscious, to live up to the divine commandments. The modern liberal is not so confident in such a direct chain of cause and effect, and in some instances, he rightly considers it an insult and a blasphemy to "explain" suffering in terms of the sins of the sufferer. The Jewish heritage looks to a messianic fulfillment of man's hopes and trusts that, in the interim, the course of history is being inexorably guided toward that end. The liberal has a vague sense of the march of human progress toward a greater degree of human justice and well-being, but he cannot imagine any end to the process, any distinct climax and transition to a perfect state of existence. He is beginning to share some of the existentialists' scruples about the objective indifference of nature to human values.

The liberal is still fundamentally optimistic about man's future. If he is becoming less confident in "the gifts of nature" or "the law of nature," he retains his hopeful picture of the corporate and even mystical entity of mankind. It is as though the totality of men embody an irresistible drive toward those many values which each man singly only partially realizes and often violates or loses entirely. Humanity takes on a corporate force of obligation, a corporate power to reward and punish, and a corporate destiny toward ever higher levels of fulfillment. The offices of Providence in Jewish theology have been appropriated by sectarian liberalism and transmuted into a religious worship of the Human Spirit. Thus, to that confidence in the uses of reason which goes back to the ancient Greeks is added that hope for the moral progress of history which goes back to the ancient Jews. And just as the devotee of the spirit of Greek rationalism must pay attention to the counterpoint of existentialism in ancient Greek thought, so the devotee of the spirit of covenant theology must pay attention to another kind of existentialist counterpoint which found its expression in ancient Israel. The Jews in biblical times were not of one mind with respect to their covenant with God. We shall seek to discover in the next chapter the entrance of a native existentialism into ancient Jewish faith and the enrichment of that faith in consequence of the challenge.

7. BIBLICAL CRISES OF FAITH

If the doctrine of the Covenant were the beginning and the end of Jewish theology, it would stand as much in opposition to existentialism as does sectarian liberalism. However, some of the subtleties which Albert Camus brought to existentialist thinking, and which go beyond a simple covenant theology, are anticipated in both the Old and again in the New Testament. As Jews and Christians wrestled with the complications and paradoxes of covenant theology in ancient times, biblical literature was fashioned into its present scope and variety. In the Holy Scriptures natively Jewish and Christian existentialist concerns come into focus and offer their challenge to liberalism.

First of all, the Bible carries the record of its peoples' doubts and questions as well as their affirmations of faith. The Preacher of Ecclesiastes, while acknowledging that God is the Lord, must also lament the vanity of all earthly existence. He dwells on the monotonous pointless motions of the natural world and on the certain destruction of all good and beautiful things. He counsels pursuit of wisdom, yet has to confess that "he who increases knowledge, increases sorrow." He alleges that "there is nothing better for a man than that he should eat and drink and find enjoyment in his toil," but he must also confess that men and beasts come to a common end and have no meaning for all their labors beyond their deaths. The Preacher is well acquainted with the variety and ingenuity of human evil, so he counsels his people to walk softly, speak little and ask no favors from life, "for a living dog is better

73

than a dead lion." There is in the Preacher a kind of urbane, mature melancholy, an acknowledgment of the burdensome and hopeless character of life and a canny sense for the temporary securities of cautious living. In its melancholy and lack of ultimate religious hope, Ecclesiastes approaches the tone of some aspects of modern existentialism and could function as a kind of low key accompaniment to Camus' *The Fall.*

The Wisdom Literature of the Bible anticipates existentialism more completely in the book of Job than in Ecclesiastes. There is neither reconciliation nor urbane resignation to evil in Job or his modern counterparts. Job is horrified by the premature loss of his felicity. He pushes to the utmost the Jewish propensity to challenge God, to strive with the Almighty, concerning the fulfillment of the divine promises. He prays to God, "Show me wherefore thou contendest with me. Is it good unto thee that thou shouldst oppress, that thou shouldst despise the work of thine hands, and shine upon the counsel of the wicked?" Such questions implying God's abrogation of the Covenant occur throughout Job's agonized self-appraisal. Although he avers that his "redeemer liveth," he feels utterly estranged from the living God and complains, "Oh that I knew where I might find him! that I might come even to his seat! I would order my cause before him, and fill my mouth with arguments." The whole twenty-third chapter ("Behold, I go forward, but he is not there; and backward, but I cannot perceive him") could serve as a suitable introduction or epigraph to Franz Kafka's existentialist novel *The Castle.* This twenty-third chapter envisages a powerful, authoritative, inescapable control of man's life, as remote and external as a feudal lord in his castle who rules his peasants from afar. Yet man has no way of finding the source of this influence or of weighing its justice or meaning. While Job carries on Israel's tradition of striving with God, he has to say of his Antagonist, "He is not a man, as I am, that I should answer him, and we should come together in judgment." In short, striving with God in the name of covenantal justice is useless. "He destroyeth the perfect and the wicked." And what seems just to a man is irrelevant to God's inscrutable purposes.

Equally existentialist in its thrust is Job's recognition that a man cannot forsake his humanity and pretend that all these great issues of good and evil, guilt and punishment, suffering and death, are ultimately trivial and have no urgency, "If I say, I will forget my complaint, I will leave off my heaviness and comfort myself: I am afraid of all my sorrows, I know that thou wilt not hold me innocent." Like the hero in Kafka's *The Trial,* Job feels unquestionably condemned and yet he has no knowledge of his Accuser or of the complaint against him.

From the point of view of Jewish piety it is to Job's everlasting credit that he never actually curses God, though his wife advises him to, and thereby suffers spiritual death. He will strive to the utmost; he will fling his unanswered questions into the sky; but he still accepts the answer out of the unredeeming whirlwind that God's ways are not his own, that he must finally resign himself to the ultimate decree. God's voice to Job describes the divine power as "king over all the children of pride." Whereupon, Job abhors himself, repents "in dust and ashes" and simply acknowledges, without further complaint, God's absolute sovereignty. Job's pride of rebellion is finally overcome; he recognizes the fruitlessness of seeking a divine perspective from which to judge human events.

Such a "reconciliation" of rebellion is no real reconciliation, but rather an abandonment of the rebel's essential protest. The utterly vague, impersonal look on the face of God which Job acknowledges, is precisely what the modern existentialist refuses to adore. If the life of man and the world are objectively cruel and ironic, let a man say so and, out of his own determination of values, curse the environing wretchedness. This is one of the twists Archibald MacLeish offers in his modern retelling of the Job story in the verse play, *J.B.* God and the Devil each wear masks. God's mask has closed eyes, its look is blank and unfeeling. The Devil's mask has wide open eyes, the power to see, confess and scorn all the unredeemable follies of man and the created world. Nickles, the Devil, quite prefers his own mask, saying, "I'd rather wear this look of loathing night after night than wear that other one—that cold complacence." Sartre's emphasis on *disgust* as a fundamental and genuinely human attitude toward the world is akin to Nickle's outlook. A man who *sees* has to be disgusted if he is to remain a man and not become an insect. If he has any therapy for his woes, it is the therapy of scorn. He is not afraid that by cursing God he will die. In fact his fear is rather that he will die if he is *not* scornfully rebellious, if he does *not* maintain his integrity in opposition to the world.

It is clear, however, that Nickles is MacLeish's devil, not his protagonist, that the therapy of scorn is not the author's final response to the mystery of evil. Neither is his answer a duplication of Job's classic resignation before Inscrutable Power. The reconciliation of the rebel to existence is a much more subtle matter, both in the Bible and in MacLeish's drama. We have said that one must look beyond a simple theology of resignation on the one hand, or simple scorn on the other. Both the Bible and MacLeish have more to say.

Not often enough has the Old Testament figure of Joseph been looked at in comparison to Job. Joseph's story, like Job's, contains certain monstrous events which could not be justified from the point of view of covenant theology—at least not until after their happy resolution. In his youth he is nearly murdered by his envious brothers. He is exiled from his family and homeland, estranged from the divine covenant and made a slave in a foreign country. In spite of his faithfulness as servant to his Egyptian master, he is falsely accused and imprisoned. Although he has fewer tangible goods to lose than did Job, he does not have the benefit of maturity to shield him from what could only appear to him as a total loss of the life into which he was born and to which, supposedly, he was divinely destined. Yet in Joseph there is none of Job's agonized questioning, no wrestling with the question of God's justice. Joseph is a kind of prototype of the suffering servant, literally and figuratively. He is estranged, and for a long time, has no tangible support save his own integrity, and a kind of unspoken faith in God's goodness. In response to the desperation into which he is cast, he utters no speeches either of protest or of false optimism. While keeping his trust in God, he does not try to escape or to justify himself by flight into Israel. The reader is simply not told what thoughts occur to Joseph concerning God's justice. He indicates no resignation to ultimate despair, but rather bears the burdens of his plight so admirably that he rises to positions of power and influence. He is free to be humanly effective because he does not waste his psychic energy in an aggressive scorn. Even though he is exiled from the destiny which had previously been promised him and his family, the energy of that promise is free to be effective within him. He seems to be convinced that God's lordship over history extends beyond the expressed limits of the covenant. Part of the transcendence of the divine will is to fulfill history in ways other than his chosen ones can anticipate. Yet when the exile is over, when Joseph is reunited with his family and when all the old physical and spiritual evils are overcome, Joseph is also free to say to his brothers: "Fear not: for am I in the place of God? But as for you, ye thought evil against me; but God meant it unto good, to bring to pass, as it is this day, to save much people alive." Joseph had never said, "If I remain faithful in my exile, God will save us all." Yet he is confident, when the unlooked-for salvation became a reality, that it was God's work.

This Old Testament image of a suffering servant represents an austere religious heritage. Fewer demands are made on God's bounty and yet sight is never lost of the ultimate benevolence of God's sovereignty over the history of mankind. Joseph is not unique in this respect. Jacob grieves for the loss of his beloved sons but does not assume that God is unjust. The forty-fourth chapter of Genesis tells how Joseph's older brother, Judah, is heroically willing to abandon his religious and political role as son of Jacob to become a slave to an Egyptian prince. In exchange for the freedom of his younger brother, Benjamin, Judah is offering his own life, following his promise to Jacob that the lad shall be brought safely home. Here especially the powerful motif of the suffering servant is invoked. Judah is not swayed by God's promise of the future prosperity of his people into abandoning his just obligation to his brother and his father. Neither does he ask for mercy, or make any loud speech to the effect that his sacrifice is God's will. His last word is simply: "How shall I go up to my father, and the lad be not with me? lest peradventure I shall see the evil that shall come on my father."

According to the Old Testament narrative, these three, Jacob, Joseph and Judah, each suffers in his own way without questioning the wisdom of God and without pious and un-knowing protestation of that wisdom and each gains a com-mon, triumphant, and unexpected relief of his woes. Their story is a kind of divine comedy, in which God's glory is seen through the recovery of meaning and hope out of the valley of despair.

In the same vein is the tale in the twenty-second chapter of Genesis of God's command to Abraham to sacrifice his only son, Isaac. Isaac stands to inherit the patriarchate from Abra-ham and with it, the promises of God's Covenant. The cruel and paradoxical command that Isaac be slain can only seem to Abraham like an absolute repudiation of the Covenant. Job's misery appears less by contrast: at least he is not required to sacrifice the life of his own son. A clue to Abraham's attitude in this most terrible crisis appears in his answer to Isaac's question, "Where is the lamb for a burnt offering?" He says, "My son, God will provide himself a lamb for a burnt offer-ing." In the literal meaning of the story, this prophecy turns out to refer to the ram which Abraham is authorized to sacri-fice in place of Isaac. But, at the level of religious symbolism, Abraham is expressing the core of reconciliation to which he has come even before the dread event. His faith tells him that God is so intimately involved in history as to suffer with his creatures the agony they suffer. "God will provide himself a lamb for a burnt offering," means that God must lose his own in the process of history and must endure the misery of it even as a parent endures the loss of his own offspring. But suffering and endurance are not the last word. Finally, the creative spirit must renew itself *because of loss* as well as in spite of it. God's suffering activates the power of renewal within himself and in all his creatures. Having endured loss from the store of his creation, he must rise with his creatures out of defeat into new creativity.

This is not the only possible reading of the Abraham and

Isaac story in the twenty-second chapter of Genesis. Rather, I bring to this story certain Christian insights I see anticipated there. Isaac is God's son as well as Abraham's, a son still living in the age of innocence and therefore appropriately symbolized as a "lamb." I understand Jesus' sonship to God in the same way, adding only that Jesus had come to maturity and had remained within the persuasion of the divine spirit to such an extent that his own and all mankind's sonship to the Father was particularly manifest in him. This beloved son must suffer and die, and with him something of the being of God must suffer and die. Metaphorically, the divine agony is a temptation to divine despair, as in the story of Noah when God decided that mankind was worthless and felt obliged to destroy all in a great flood. Such "despair" is only temporary. Inexorably the sacrifice is followed by renewal. As God set the rainbow of hope and salvation in Noah's stormy sky, so the Disciples rose up from defeat to be the church. A new burst of human and divine creativity and freedom follows hard upon the terrible ordeal. After Jesus' death the recovery of his followers recaptures his essential power and magnifies and disseminates it among all men; the ending is finer than the beginning. In this sense do I understand the symbolism of resurrection.

This is not to say that ordeals are to be invited for the sake of resurrections. Jesus' agony was terrible and its terror is not to be explained away by the good that followed. But, given the ordeals, the Creative Life of God responds in all his creatures toward reconciliation and renewal. For as God suffers with his sons, and as his creatures know of this cosuffering, they are hopeful of the power of creative resurrection. It is almost as though Abraham and Jesus, sensing the love of God, were each able to forgive the Almighty for the harsh and inexplicable necessities of an imperfect life and world; and by forgiveness they could trust in a mysterious renewal beyond what appeared to be ultimate catastrophe.

The church's conventional imagery of God's absolute sovereignty tends to block the interpretation we have been discussing. A God literally responsible for every last turn of events would not be likely to impose upon himself conditions of sacrifice and suffering. In the biblical stories there is a more naive, yet truer picture of the divine agency. God grants some freedom of decision to his creatures, and with this freedom comes the power to rebel, to destroy, to fail. The precious gift of freedom cannot be abrogated merely to put an end to failure and suffering. Freedom of the creature is testimony both to the wisdom of God and to his liability to suffering. And man, the beneficiary both of human freedom and divine love, is forced to learn that he possesses these gifts by paying the price of dwelling in an imperfect world. He cannot have the gift of freedom and love without the consequence of evil. And even as he is called to rebel against every particular imperfection, he is also called upon to be reconciled to the continuing necessity for imperfection. Man, in a metaphorical sense, must not only thank God for the gifts of life but also forgive God for its evil even as he struggles against particular evils.

A passage in MacLeish's *J.B.* makes just this point. In arguing with his wife against her counsel of despair, J.B. says:

> God is there, too, in the desperation.
> I do not know why God should strike
> But God is what is stricken also:
> Life is what despairs in death
> And, desperate, is life still.

To me this is a more profound biblical insight than the affirmation occurring at the end of the play where J.B. and his wife confess to each other that their only hope comes from the love in their own hearts. At the end of his play MacLeish loses the image of the divine Cosufferer and one is left with the pathetic picture of the two loved ones hopelessly pitted against a totally indifferent world. It may be that this more obviously existentialist conclusion is the one the author wishes to convey. From the point of view of the Judeo-Christian tradition, a greater wisdom was momentarily revealed earlier in the play. It is worthy of note that Mr. Zuss, MacLeish's image of the conventional deity and counterpart to Nickles, the conventional Devil, is shocked to hear J.B. forgive God in the passage just quoted. It had not occurred to Zuss (nor does it occur to any-

one who fails to question the doctrine of absolute divine sovereignty) that God should ever be in need of forgiveness.
Nevertheless, I submit that some such metaphor is an integral
part of biblical theology.

The New Testament continues the same shocking witness
by suggesting that, through Jesus, God suffered among men
and deserves man's compassion. This seems to me the real
stumbling block to Greek conceptions of divine imperturba-
bility or to Jewish monarchical conceptions of divine omnip-
otence. Yet the Jews are equipped, by the very imagery of
their tradition, to acknowledge the ways in which the Lord of
History suffers with and is reconciled to his choicest champions.
Abraham, Jacob, Joseph, Moses, Jesus and Paul, all had their
agonies and (especially Moses) their agonized questions and
strivings against the Lord. But not one of them followed the
purely existentialist pattern of scorning God and the world
for its miseries. These wanderers were all blithe spirits, maintaining in the midst of cruel realities an irrepressible hope and
an ever-renewing power for constructive action. To use the
language of Camus (in contrast to the language of more
orthodox existentialism), they accepted the fact of Plague and,
in humble reconciliation to the inevitable, they set aside
despair and addressed themselves to redeeming whatever they
could. Man must find means of forgiving not only his brother,
whom he has seen, but also the very conditions of his existence,
which are largely invisible and intangible. His only alternative
is despair and the deadly illusion that scorn is therapeutic. St.
Paul has put the point most concisely—"For godly sorrow
worketh repentance to salvation not to be repented of: but the
sorrow of the world worketh death."

Both existentialism and certain aspects of Jewish and
Christian teaching repudiate simple covenant theology which
decrees that man is to be rewarded in every instance for his
righteousness. They also repudiate sectarian liberalism insofar
as it postulates a harmony between human goodness and the
natural world. Neither covenant theology nor liberalism can
be said to be in all respects wrong; but both must be seriously
qualified. Thus liberalism in its usual form must respond

earnestly to a twofold challenge: there is the somber challenge of straight-line existentialism with its Hellenic melancholy and its Job-like rage at the monstrosities of reality; and there is the bright challenge of Jewish and Christian compassion with its sense of reconciliation to the heart of life through human and divine suffering. Either the existentialist "sorrow of the world" or the biblical "godly sorrow" makes a claim upon every man today. A self-reforming liberalism will not fear to acknowledge and respond to both these claims.

8. CHRISTIAN AFFIRMATIONS

A peculiar *rapprochement* between Christianity and the existentialist pathos occurs in the imagery of the Crucifixion. Here is no noble tragedy, no grand agony in the Greek tradition replete with heroic oratory. Jesus was miserably lynched, and he died in utter abandonment by those very persons who should have stood with him. Of course, the figure of Jesus is anything but pathetic up to the time of his final ordeal. But the peculiar power of the Christian witness is its direct confrontation of the question of the wreckage of human hopes and values by the juggernaut of mass hostility and mob violence. The Gospels anticipate the modern agony and penetrate far into the meanings of this peculiarly miserable kind of human experience.

It ought, therefore, to be true that secular existentialists and Christians would easily communicate with and fortify one another. Unfortunately, such is not the case. The whole theological background of Christianity appears inaccessible to existentialism. Christ on the Cross may carry an immediate and authentic message for the existentialist; Christ Risen does not. The "sorrow of the world" in the existentialist consciousness argues for human endurance and creativity without any ultimate or transcendent hope.

There seem to be some liberal churchmen and ministers who find themselves close to the same kind of despair. They have become disaffected from the hopes of sectarian liberalism as well as from those of the biblical heritage. In such instances, one's only alternative—and a grim one it is—is to resort to something akin to the melancholy of the Greeks. It means struggling without hope, waiting for the future to reveal new, temporary sources of creativity while refusing to become involved in what is regarded as a dead and confining past. There is something admirable about such a "waiting" religion with its astringent forms and its constant guard against any lapse into alleged superstition. But its practitioners should be warned that their enforced exile, if extended, will result in the collapse of their church as an institution. What may be temporarily plausible and necessary can end in self-destruction. Every institution, including a church, needs some basis of communal understanding and action, some center of energy, and a stable platform for the launching of activity if it is to survive. Spiritual emptiness, especially when enshrined in an institution, is an invitation to suspicion, contention and dissolution among its members.

For these reasons the liberal church will be helped if it can cast away sufficiently its local biases and native emotional blocks, at least enough to look candidly and not uncritically at the positive challenges of Christian faith. All of this is not to say that either sectarian liberalism or existentialism are completely invalid. It is to say, rather, that they are incomplete and vulnerable as long as they disregard the strength deeply embedded in the foundations of Western culture by virtue of the Christian heritage.

Before turning to the more concrete aspects of Christianity, it is desirable to entertain certain philosophical considerations. Throughout, our method of inquiry has been that of philosophical theology, which allows no priority of authority either to the concretions of a particular faith or to the abstractions of a more general system. Paraphrasing Kant, every concrete faith without logical and systematic integration is blind, and every system without vivid, concrete vehicles of expression is empty. In the present stage of our argument certain general presuppositions and attitudes should be made clear.

Western philosophical thought, under the dominance of Plato, Aristotle, Aquinas and Spinoza has been largely monistic. The overwhelming singularity and centrality of the universe has taken precedence over every impression of stubborn, irreducible fact. Individual things, and the mental facts supporting them, have been considered real only as derivative from and controlled by a supervening Unity. The monism of the Greeks combined with the Jewish conception of the absolute authority of God created, in the Christian Middle Ages and later, the image of a closed universe ultimately intolerant of the deviations and freedom of any of its parts. Some such image haunts the grosser processes of science to this day, where it is assumed that events are to be understood only as consequences of previous events in an ultimately unified system. As the complexity of science becomes daily more apparent, the goal of one unified science recedes in probability, perhaps even in possibility.

Meanwhile, in spite of the ambition of rational man to see reality as truly and ultimately one, common sense and daily experience are forever bombarded by the stubborn plurality and unpredictability of phenomena. Nature is real; and nature has many parts, many of which carry on a semi-independent existence and a sporadic or persistent conflict among one another. What is called the inescapable margin of freedom in man is called "spontaneity" at the subhuman levels of phenomena. William James, Peirce, Bergson and Whitehead all found ways of attributing to all the parts of experienced reality qualities variously connoted by such words as chance, emergence, spontaneity or freedom. The classical penchant for absolute order has given way to the picture of a more disorderly universe. James's title to one of his own books quite bluntly states the paradox of "A Pluralistic Universe." Scientists can participate in the same outlook if they recognize a principle of indeterminacy in reality and a condition of ultimate discoordination of their own efforts in spite of local areas of harmonious explanation.

Philosophic cosmology today is considerably more dynamic as a result of the breakdown of absolute monistic systems. The Heraclitean spirit prevails; the universe is seen to be endlessly restless. Whether this restlessness is hopefully progressive, as it tends to be in a doctrine of evolution, or whether it is thought to have no ultimate meaning or goal in its unceasing transformations, we remain aware of being caught up in a moving reality. The experience of flux is given an optimistic evaluation through the term "creativity." The constant emergence of new entities and new forms of being is attributed, in Whitehead's metaphysics, to human and natural creativity. H. N. Wieman has understood the nature of the divine primarily under the rubric of continuing creativity. What is less often discussed in these connections is the cost of creativity, i.e., that spontaneity can lead to discoordination, that a creative universe can engender chaos. Using a familiar political image, one may wonder whether any universe so conceived and so dedicated can long endure. The spontaneity of the parts of creation and the limited degree of harmonious coordination throughout, calls into question the absolute authority of any alleged divine ruler and threatens with ultimate dissolution what now appears to be a single universe. The possibility of tragedy, at least in principle, is thus imputed to vaster realms of being than the life of man. Any theology which takes creativity and spontaneity seriously will necessarily abandon the image of God as one who is in complete control of events down to the last blade of grass ruffled by a casual wind. If divine sovereignty is to mean anything at all, it must allow for real rebellions against itself, nor can it foresee in every detail the future resolutions of spontaneous conflict.

How are these conflicts in human and natural experience "solved"? We may generalize and say that those vitalities which survive in a given instance of destruction find new modes of cooperation and growth when no escape or transfer is available or the destruction spreads. It is at the level of finding new modes of cooperation and growth that creativity (whether conceived naturalistically or theologically) is most significant. Creativity is not simply a new birth; it is that indefatigable energy and wisdom whereby the very conditions of breakdown and decay become material and setting for regeneration. Theologically, this means that creativity is primarily redemptive. Whitehead uses the figure of "persuasion" as being most characteristic of the innermost nature of all divine process. The unity of all events consists mainly in a power of improvisation, wherein things which seem to work against one another can find new ways of coexistence and mutual improvement. Every breakdown of form, from physical decay to human tragedy, contains the potential for the renewal of meaning even beyond the level of the original form. This is not "the best of all possible worlds." What good there is lies in the power to transform for better and greater that which had been moving toward worse and less. Our universe is essentially experimental; and its deepest "wisdom" is to use what appears to be failure as the platform from which to launch new forms of creation.

When we speak of the "wisdom" of the universe we move away from philosophical language toward the theological. We are dealing here with processes which can be observed only in part, whose full value and cause remain mysterious. Accordingly, we must resort to theological language lest the richness of the mystery be unvoiced. The image of God in the Christian heritage, without sacrificing the magnificence and awesome quality of its Old Testament symbols, has acquired new and more subtle dimensions in Christian theology. These deepening themes have been expressed by such metaphors as reconciliation and forgiveness—of man toward his fellow man, of God toward man, and even of man toward God. We saw in the previous chapter how these images are anticipated in certain Old Testament stories and how they are suggested in Archibald MacLeish's modern retelling of the Job story. It is the unique power of the Christian heritage to emphasize and dramatize these themes and thus to reveal the divine share in a network of forgiveness and reconciliation by which Creativity is believed to be eternal. This contribution of the Christian witness does no more than extend and supplement the basic optimism of the Jews who, throughout their tragic history, did not lose faith in the Great Renewer.

The essential Christian concern is that God is fully immanent as well as removed; and immanent means to be incarnate, to be present and active in the very flesh and stuff of experience. This is itself a shocking conception to the Greek philosophical mind. For a Greek such as Plato, flesh and stuff are ephemeral, changeable and utterly fallible in their susceptibility to imperfection and suffering. The Divine, by contrast, is pure, unperturbed, and serenely changeless. Man's intellect strives to make contact with the upper or spiritual region and thus save some part of himself from the inevitable onset of decay and death in the lower or terrestrial region. In dividing reality, Plato was nourished religiously by the Orphic mystery cults. It was an affront to all such Hellenism when Christians said that God was directly manifest in the human flesh of Jesus Christ. To be incarnate is to take on the burdens and ambiguities of finite existence. The very being of God is seen to participate in the improvisations of spontaneous process and to suffer the pain of separation and estrangement as well as the joy of loving harmony.

Orthodox Christianity goes on to assert that this peculiar joining of the human and the divine in the Incarnate Lord occurred solely and uniquely in Jesus Christ and that man benefits only adventitiously from this totally singular event. A belief in such derivation of spiritual power from a vicarious source depends heavily upon the extension of faith or superstition beyond life and process as experienced and known. What can be the application of an absolutely unique phenomenon to the commonplace pattern of daily living? Would it not be better to argue that the doctrines of cocreation and cosuffering (which are found both in the Old Testament and in process philosophy) extend to all men in all situations? For every creature is God incarnate, is expressive of the divine creative energy, and also is a spontaneous event potentially self-estranging from its own center. This means that man and God rejoice concurrently in the achievement of new creative harmonies and suffer concurrently in the breakdown of former harmonies. Christ becomes a prototype of that divine Love which belongs to and unites all creatures but which, at the same time, must grieve at the gates of Jerusalem, must go among the sick and dying, dwell in the presence of weakness and perfidy, and suffer the agony of death itself. Christ is our earnest of the hope that the Power which renders our being possible and actual, also endures with us the diminution of Itself in the decay or destruction of ourselves.

Out of such intimately shared creative and destructive processes one may derive the meaning of forgiveness on a human and transhuman level. A man becomes reconciled to his brother; an evil condition finds the power to recover from its evil. The power of recovery in both cases stems from the very powers which precipitated the original disruption. The regeneration expresses in small compass what seems to occur throughout all reality. Nothing is perfect and chaos is legion. But Creativity, God, God-incarnate, all connote a loving, persuasive, and unifying core to the multiplicity of things—a core which is endlessly inventive in joining estranged parts and improvising from the wrecks of the past the new forms of the present and future.

The metaphor of Divine Love can be used in several ways. Love as the Author of multiplicity provides for that very estrangement of parts which makes love as we know it possible. For love requires some distance between that which loves and is loved. Creation is estrangement for the sake of the possibility of love. The image of divine incarnation is that very image of self-estrangement in God. He who is all in all is also within the creatures, agent and power of their own creativity, the very multiplicity in which, by the bonds of love, the Unity rejoices. But to share in created multiplicity is to take on the burden of estrangement as well as the joy of loving harmony. God suffers with his creatures in their conflicts and partial chaos, just as the whole person suffers with some diseased part of his body. The power of cosuffering is also the power of redemption. For as there is in Christian thought no absolute power outside of God to destroy him, so the pain of cosuffering is an immediate spur to remedial energies and restorative powers. Suffering elicits the drive toward healing and reconstruction. It is in this context that religious sages have believed suffering to be the key to wisdom. As a man suffers, so he participates in the great struggle for life and harmony everywhere and comes to recognize a communal reality binding all men and ultimately all things.

It will be noted, of course, that suffering embitters perhaps about as often as it enlightens. At this important crossroads, the power of forgiveness is essential. Unless a man can forgive the conditions of his suffering, no matter how intense his own special indignations and hostilities, he cannot lay hold of the cocreative power for reconciliation and renewal. Ultimate scorn in face of suffering is ultimate estrangement, and this is actually inconceivable except in terms of suicide. Albert Camus' question about the ultimate seriousness of suicide implies that if there is truly no basis of harmony in human existence, then life itself is forfeit. Anger, hostility, scorn are all part of estrangement; they are the negative side of love which also must operate among a true separateness and plurality of events. But ultimate anger—that is, estrangement without a shred of forgiveness—is ultimate isolation, or bluntly speaking, death.

That Creative Power which brings forth the unified multiplicity of created things must, metaphorically speaking, endure, forgive, and be reconciled to, the evil effects of its own inner spontaneity and diversity. Without this risk and without its reconciling inner forgiveness, how could the universal Love be possible? Love is not real unless forgiveness is real.

These many themes and concerns find their focus in Christian imagery. The mercy of man toward the imperfections of himself and his existence constitute the ultimate source of power. This mercy—through the picture of the divine-humanity of Christ—is imputed to all existence and leads to that metaphor of redemption whereby creativity is maintained and advanced. Christ asks God to forgive those who, in their anxiety and hostility, "know not what they do." By his forgiveness, Christ restores to life and power persons whom society has utterly cast out. Most of all, by accepting as finally inevitable his own cruel fate, Christ implies forgiveness of his Creator. He does not direct against either man or God the scornful rebellion characteristic of the modern existentialist, or that unreal sense of personal nobility characteristic of the sectarian liberal. He enters into the miserable as well as exalted moments of his fellow men and by the power of acceptance, mercy, forgiveness, reconciliation, leaves a permanent new reality and hope across the face of the planet.

Our search for clarity in these matters must include patience with the mystery. And perhaps the greatest mystery of which we have been speaking is that man can show forgiveness and acceptance toward the totality of his existence precisely because the Author of that totality is incarnate within him. Man takes his cue from the Creator whose cocreator and cosufferer he is. And the redemption from suffering and evil which man experiences is not from "on high" but mediated directly through the flesh of his companions and their communal bonds to the materials of the natural world. Thus Christ is all men who, *in extremis,* forgive their Creator, their world and their fellow men for the pathos and tragedies of their lives. With such reconciliation there is creativity. Therefore, Christ is all men who, *in extremis,* bequeath to the future the power of recovery and renewal even as they themselves die in the process of its unfolding. Each creature's bond to the whole must be broken and terminated by death. The God in each creature is renewed by the degree to which that creature accepts his fate and builds *as though he were immortal.* Here the spontaneity of man is joined with the eternal power of God. Whether by creativity or in suffering, such united power is the expression of Love in God and man.

Although Christ is thus supremely what all men can potentially be and although he is a living incarnation of God, he does not exhaust all possible facets of the meaning of the divine reality. God could certainly not be God and be less than Christ. The Creator of Heaven and Earth must also extend beyond what any man, Christ or otherwise, can know or reveal. Neither our thought nor our imagination, nor any combination of these in any act of faith, traverses to the end of the universe or sees all things whole. We see Holiness but not the Whole. And Christ himself is transparent for a Magnificence that transcends him.

In answer to the limitations of sectarian liberalism or to the scorn and despair of existentialism, the imagery and reality of Christ, cocreating and cosuffering with God, remains to challenge and haunt the religious seeker. The inheritance of Christianity is piled high with distortions and abuses; and, considering the varying perspectives of men, some of the foregoing paragraphs will seem distorted to many who call themselves Christian. The "unity" of Christendom can never be creedal. It can only be a common acknowledgment that the person of Christ, his existential power, his freedom, and his persistent teaching, deserves to haunt the intelligence and imagination with its manifold enigmas. To follow Christ means, minimally, to *be concerned,* to be fascinated by his reality and to be continually brought back to his commentary on the human condition and its implied hope for the future of man. Every devotee of liberal religion, while concerned with the Christian witness, must be and finally is free in all specific decisions of faith and action. The gift of Christ is also man's opportunity for free response.

9. THE VALIDITY OF THEOLOGICAL LANGUAGE

The demands of religious openness require that every liberal religious inquirer not flatly reject his heritage. Hopefully, he can avoid the prejudices that his times are unique, that he need never refer to the past for spiritual guidance, and that all hope is to be vested in totally new discoveries, new approaches and new modes of expression. Significant novelty is not found solely in utter isolation from the past. Rather, it is *significant* because it joins one to a past from which he had seemed to be alienated. It is *novel* because it pours into the reappropriated past contemporary experience and coloration. Its power arises from the conviction that the task of the present is "not to destroy the law" but to fulfill it.

Although one may maintain that liberalism should reform itself by novel reappropriation of its religious heritage, the road to such reform is often beset by serious semantic blocks. The biblical heritage is conveyed through concrete theological symbolism. The resolution of the tension between man's hope and man's despair is expressed through stories of dramatic encounters between God and man. Even if one is disposed to believe that there is in the stuff of existence an ultimate resource for personal strength and corporate health, one may not be equally disposed to accept this reality in the personal and anthropomorphic forms of its original myths. One may acknowledge that certain myths are exciting dramatic symbols of human rescue and renewal, but their very *symbolic* character may block the belief in an existential relationship to the divine reality purportedly described. It is one thing to be an external witness to some kind of poetry of salvation; it is another to be free to address one's own prayers meaningfully to a living God.

93

In these dilemmas the modern religious liberal shares common ground with the modern secular existentialist. The story of Jesus' suffering and crucifixion is devastatingly authentic, while his resurrection seems unrealistic and wishful. A similar contrast must be acknowledged in the Old Testament. Abraham's ordeal leading to the sacrifice of his son seems more plausible in primitive society than the angelic voice which stays his knife. We respond favorably to Moses' courage in facing Pharaoh and demanding freedom, but we do not understand the miracle of divine support in the Plagues and in the crossing of the Red Sea. Job's agony has touched the sympathy of modern readers, but his restoration to happiness at the end of the story seems to lack realism and authenticity. All these tales look finally to an anthropomorphically expressed divine agency for rescue and renewal. But the difficulty of believing in any kind of rescue and renewal renders the Good News of divine grace doubly unauthentic.

If this sense of unauthenticity derives not from objections to mythological phraseology but from a more basically pessimistic view of human life relief can best be found in acts of human sympathy and support. But if, as is the case with most liberals, there exists a substratum of optimism and a disposition to acknowledge the reality of human recovery, then the message of the Bible ought to be recognized as supporting and sustaining such belief, not as discouraging or frustrating it. If such recognition does not occur, one must ask whether the block to understanding arises from the seeming invalidity of theological language as such. One who has long been used to thinking of reality in impersonal terms will not respond favorably to the Bible's image of a personal deity with whom a man may converse in worship and prayer. If he can think of God at all, he pictures a mysteriously pervasive yet impersonal reality, a power to be worked with, not a Person to be prayed to. Others may envy the solace and security of biblical faith, but they appear to be constitutionally unable to project themselves into such a state of mind. They would like to pray but honestly cannot. Having been nurtured on conceptions of a scientific reality, the words stick in their throats. They can see no meaning to addressing sentences to an unknown Auditor somewhere in the darkness. The reality of the Bible's picture of God has withered not so much through the force of argument as through the slow attrition of disuse until it has become irrelevant or meaningless. The language and imagery of the Bible seem increasingly out of joint with modern times.

Our concern with biblical language should not be taken as a substitute for faith or the lack of it. To try to interpret the intent and symbolic power of biblical speech is not to create that power; it is only to help people find it for themselves where, otherwise, they might be blocked from looking for it or from taking it seriously. In the present chapter we are seeking, at best, a doorway to affirmation through which the intellectually concerned may walk without stooping and without a feeling of compromise.

What then, may we reasonably conclude about the nature and validity of biblical language? It is the language of poetry; it is also the language of divine-human communion. There can be no sense of communion without the resources of poetry, but poetry is not in itself religious communion. In the Bible, the language of poetry and the language of communion imply each other; and the latter, while built upon the former, transcends it. After we have described the poetic dimension of biblical symbolism, we shall move through poetry and beyond it to what Buber calls the "meeting" of man and God.

Consider the love of the poet for the object of his poem. Is this enthusiasm in the poet's mind and body? Is his ecstasy something wholly subjective and limited to himself? Does he project a vitality and a sense of values that has no real counterpart in his environment, that is purely the product of his own emotions? I think the answer is no. It is quite arbitrary, even dogmatic, to conclude that the grace and beauty of the rose dwell only in the poet's eye, as though the true rose were a thing only of molecules and measurement. It is true that until the poet sees and reacts, the rose would never be understood in the poetic way. But in back of the description is the reality; and unless the rose had the substance to inspire the poet and stimulate the poetic art, the poem could never have been written. All this is to assert that the world is worthy of the fervor which dwells alike in poetry itself and in the poetic dimension of religion. The depth of existence stimulates both the art of the poet and the prayer of the worshiper. These responses partake of the subjectivity, the local color and character of both poet and worshiper, but they are neither pure invention nor "mere" symbol. They are reflections of a real power, a real loveliness, a real magnificence.

Because the poet and worshiper must bring their own power of response to the object, and because Western culture has tended to enshrine the methods of neutral measurement rather than partisan poetics, it is not surprising that our attitude tends to be reductionistic. We say reality is "no more than" what appears to the scientist, that the poet's evaluations are superadded. Does not a consistent reductionism require that the strictures placed on the poet be extended also to the scientist? We acknowledge that something in the richness and order of reality is reflected in the findings of science, granting at the same time that this "something" transcends any one scientific description or all such descriptions taken together. Science lives and thrives on a philosophy of abundance rather than on a philosophy of reduction; there is always *more* for the scientist to find out.

Consistency dictates that we say the same of poetry. There is always *more* for the poet to discover; and every great achievement in poetry deepens the sense of the infinite fullness of reality and the need for further poetic penetration. The penetration of the poet is aimed not at an atomistic analysis of phenomena, but at the synthetic re-presentation of units of experience at an intensified level of vitality. The poet recaptures and heightens the impact of immediate experience. He does so in such a way as not to reduce experience exclusively to his dramatic or lyrical categories, but rather to suggest a power extending beyond what he has explicitly expressed. He is fundamentally a witness to power and loveliness, not a neutral measurer of component parts.

As poetry, the Bible achieves a similar effect. The lyrical and stately attribution of the elements of our experience to the magnificent bounty of God is one way of eliciting a sense of their innate value. The holiness which the poet grasps piecemeal in his attention to particular phenomena is affirmed to be one mighty and multiform power proceeding out of infinite mystery and manifested in sudden explosions or subtle arrivals of glory.

"The world is charged with the grandeur of God," says Gerard Manley Hopkins, a grandeur which sometimes "will flame out like shining from shook foil" and sometimes "will gather like the ooze of oil crushed." The psalmist, using the metaphor of the eloquence of nature, says "The heavens declare the glory of God. . . . Day unto day uttereth speech." He resorts to the imagery of the dance as in "The mountain skipped like rams and the little hills like lambs." A poetic expression of terror and emptiness is as likely as an ecstasy of joy, "And the wild beasts of the islands shall cry in their desolate houses, and dragons in their pleasant palaces." The vengeance of the Lord is described thus: "for the windows from on high are open and the foundations of the earth do shake." The trumpets and drums of judgment are supplemented by the clear sound of hope, as the prophet Isaiah sings, "Ye shall have a song, as in the night when a holy solemnity is kept; and gladness of heart, as when one goeth with a pipe to come into the mountain of the Lord, to the mighty one of Israel."

In the many moods of biblical poetry all qualities of dramatic and lyrical value are found coursing through the world, including and transcending the being of man. Man's deep enthusiasms and aversions are not limited to his own reality; he derives his passions, his loves, fears and serene joys, from the whole complex of realities in which he is involved. His music is partly his own and partly derived from beyond him, but he can never be certain which part is which. As poet and worshiper he creates by his own artistic invention adequate though imperfect symbols for the manifold holiness in which he dwells. The excellence of his invention is in direct proportion to his power to respond to the vitality of his God-filled world. He sees this world not as an aggregate of neutral substances to be analyzed according to their local influences and interactions, but rather as a community of creatures, each reflecting the Creator's glory but none being the perfect fulfillment. This is to say, with Tillich, that the manifest beauty and power in particular things points beyond itself to the Power of Being by which each thing is created and sustained. Through the energy of poetry, as well as in direct experience, finite beings appear to reflect Being Itself though they are never equivalent to it. One loves not only other men but also the created world through its many quasi-personal creatures. Through the poetry of the Bible, one can approach *communion with* rather than mere *detached examination of* all parts of the world.

The mention of communion brings us to certain philosophical and theological questions about biblical language. Even granting that poetic evaluations are responses to real values in the world, how can the poetry of religion claim to be a witness to an *actual* transcendent Reality? Why not say that the ecstatic speech of psalmist and prophet is simply their peculiarly theological way of placing highest value on the world? Could we not argue that the Bible points to no divine reality, to no objective Holiness, but only to the richness of the world which the poetic imagination of the biblical authors has constructed into a Being? Further, why not say that they connote that richness by attributing it to (and therefore attributing *to it*) an infinite glory? The language of prayer and thanksgiving would then be seen as the literary device of hyperbole—a way of placing highest evaluation upon certain objects of experience.

The foregoing suggestions may appeal as a way to explain away the theological claims of religion. But the intent of biblical language and the language of worship is otherwise. The attribution of God's holiness to creation is not offered solely in order that we may love the creatures better. It is offered that we may commune directly with the Creator. The language of prayer is the language of communion as well as the language of poetic evaluation. He who prays speaks to God, and to speak to God is something more than speaking poetically about his works.

A principal problem relating to the idea of communion with deity is our tendency to think of communion as a purely human act. Man can address all the world, but only another man seems capable of replying. Unless the general character of the world can show some aptitude for intercommunion, it becomes meaningless to talk about the whole as capable of partaking in some kind of communion with man. If the Bible's image of God as quasi-personal and communicable is to make sense, it is only because there is some kind of communion between man and nature. Our concern here is not to present "arguments for the existence of God." Rather, it is to show that the activity of communion with God in prayer is not wholly unique and esoteric, but an extension of a possible fundamental relationship with finite realities.

How shall we ultimately describe that collection of finite realities in which we dwell and which we call the natural world? Shall we be limited to the old model of a collection of atoms or of certain final subatomic particles, particles which are utterly blind, unfeeling, and neutral in quality? And shall we then say that all the complexity of observed phenomena, ourselves included, is achieved by different external "arrangements" of the subatomic building blocks? I do not think that any such model makes sense. The complexity of the world involves distinctions in quality—not only man's intellectual distinctions, but also that perceived selectivity whereby one phenomenon fares in such and such ways in a given situation and differently in different situations. The varieties of selectivity in natural process are ultimately mysterious in origin. But we can say more about them than is implied in the model of neutral building blocks variously arranged. To oversimplify the matter, a bag of marbles yields nothing but a collection of spheres no matter how often one shakes them up and rearranges their relative positions. The marbles remain external to one another and can change one another only by causing destruction, by a mutual shattering. They are impotent to expand and increase qualitative differences.

A model more biological in quality is called for even at the atomic and subatomic level. We can extend the character of rudimentary feeling, of challenge and response to feeling, to every part of existence. "Feeling" should be understood as broadly as possible and should include more than that peculiar form of sentience characteristic of the central nervous system of animals. Although "feeling" is a biological model, it is used here to indicate the way any organic or inorganic event selectively holds its own multiple parts together. Certain qualities are realized and alternatives are ruled out. This central feeling pattern is a form of subjectivity, whether rudimentary or complex; it is an attraction toward or repulsion from various other kinds or centers of being and feeling. Small events are also citizens in the societies of larger events. The smaller event exhibits an inner drive whose teleology is influenced by the "feeling-choices," i.e., the attractions and repulsions of the larger societies in which it resides. The influence of one event by another springs from a process of mutual or symbiotic sensitivity which yields subjective unity. Each thing must construe the data of an object given to it in a way somewhat similar to the way that object has in turn construed *its* own previous data. Otherwise, there would be no continuity in time, no mutual influence or causality. I cannot eat a stone because I cannot construe the data of stoniness the way stones actually do. I must select by my own feelings some object such as a peach or apple which in turn has felt and selected its data in a way native to my subjectivity.

In this model of "feeling of feeling" we are following and oversimplifying Whitehead's philosophy of organism, which Hartshorne has further developed and described as "contributionism." The basic model for reality is organic. Societies of events are included within one another and, by limited spontaneity and selectivity, events "choose" or "shun" one another, thus fading into and emerging out of one another in continual process. Causality is internal as well as external; it is feelingful as well as blind; it is universally subjective as well as objective. Objects are subject to the causality, to being the data of the larger societies which they inhabit. Objects are also subjects, centers of spontaneous activity from inner impulse, capable of construing other subjects as objects or data for themselves.

There is a vast difference between the rudimentary and spontaneous attractions and repulsions of the electrons and the highly complex attractions and repulsions of human consciousness and freedom. But there is no absolute difference. Man belongs to nature. Man also is unique in nature just as every part of nature has some uniqueness from the whole. Uniqueness may be no more than the tiny spontaneity of an electron in the vast monotony of atomic process. Uniqueness may be as striking as Shakespeare's personal creativity. Both forms of uniqueness are real and not wholly unrelated, the smaller and the larger.

In ways generally analogous to human consciousness but vastly different in detail, all events feel their world in determinate fashion and by the selectivity of their feeling they construe their data according to various patterns. Thus, they become what they are in contradistinction to what they are not. We are using this model of feeling of feeling—a vast network of intercommunion in nature—as the basis for the conviction that the poet and artist feel the subjectivity, the telos or inner aim of their objects and express this relationship in quasi-personal terms. The poet feels his object as a subject to be addressed and not as a thing to be dismembered and used in some altered form. And similarly, we say that the man who prays is encountering the feeling of the largest event wherein all other events are contained. Man is a part of the society of the universe and, for all its diversity, man also has intuited that it is literally a *uni*verse. He can commune with its unity and centrality by virtue of his membership in it.

Religious communion occurs when man realizes that his own intelligence belongs to an intercommunicative whole, that human feeling is an instance of that single complexity which creates and vastly transcends all that man is. His use of personal language in prayer and worship is his own native and unique way of expressing communion. Man's sense of the immediacy and richness of the Whole stems from the verbal and personal communion he has with it, and from ways more subtle than man's limited understanding can imagine. Not that God answers prayer in so many words in the correct language. Rather we are saying that God contains and absorbs the whole of man, including his prayers, and responds as wisely and lovingly to the spontaneities and offerings of man as He does to the spontaneities and offerings of all of nature. God is the one dimension of being that responds to man more richly and completely than any other, more richly even than man himself. All man's other actions toward nature transcend those affected. Thus, God becomes a personal reality to an extent that surpasses our most active imaginations.

The language of sympathy and communion better expresses the intuition of interrelatedness throughout reality than the models of impersonal Wisdom, Law of Nature, Harmony, Chance, etc. The non-feeling world picture isolates man's valuations and thought processes as exceptions to a vast rule of impersonality or, what is worse, purports to reduce the human functions to the non-human. Our age tends constantly to reduce human nature. It is the task of religion in our age to preserve an image of human personality and to bring nature closer to it. Further, religion must free man for the fullest expression of his personality in his relation to God. Organic and teleological thinking is optimistic in epistemology and theology. It says that we sense our world and our God because of a basic affinity coursing through and binding all worlds and God. The world is upgraded toward our own complexity and richness. And God, for all his transcendence, also participates in the qualities of our human finitude.

It is for the foregoing reasons that I consider the biblical language of communion between man and his Creator to have meaning for man's thought and action. The reasonableness of prayer is real and makes the act of prayer real and significant. The Bible presents stories of men who felt this relationship to divinity and built the drama of their lives upon it. The poetic description is just one notable part of the Bible. It is also a religious account of many divine-human encounters which have occurred in the forms of creation, judgment and redemption.

Let it also be admitted that the language of the Bible invites certain kinds of misunderstanding and error. Its dramas are sometimes so precisely conceived as to make divine action seem overly human. God is described as molding man from the dust of the ground and breathing into his nostrils the breath of life. In the hands of fundamentalists such anthropomorphic doctrines have been used to oppose modern biological science. Any humanizing of God runs the risk of making religion a tool of a priesthood and not a genuine stance before a transcendent and judging Holiness. Apparently some of the biblical writers were aware of this danger, for the Bible is unique in the literature of religion as providing correctives for its own potential abuses. The ancient Jewish prophets and seers were loathe to give any visual description of God. They wrote of him either in the guise of an angelic messenger or more often as an invisible voice coming out of clouds or dazzling light. His manifestations to Jacob and Joseph were generally dreams. His coming to Moses was in clouds and fire. His glory manifested in the temple to Isaiah was a radiance in which all form was dissolved. Even in the story of Creation in the first chapter of Genesis, we are told nothing of who God was or how he worked, but only that his mysterious Word went forth and the world arose like a beautiful bride in response. A word is at once specific, meaningful, and also invisible and transcendent in its being. The biblical authors had the wisdom to protect their references to God from overly explicit imagery. The Bible has built into its very narratives the energy to resist idolatry and the realization that the Creator-Redeemer is infinite and transcendent.

All of this points to the fact that the personal imagery of religion is subject to the fallibilities of human behavior and must be guarded and purified as much from within the religious framework as from outside it. Above all, religion must be wary of the destructive attitude that God is no more than a person to be manipulated. The retention of impersonal as well as personal imagery is one protective factor. God is pictured as nearer than hands and feet, as manifest through seers and prophets and in Christ, but yet as the great Abyss, the Unconditional, the Infinite Mystery. Without this austere element of distance and judgment, religion tends (using Whitehead's phrase) to "degenerate into a decent formula wherewith to embellish a comfortable life." Without the personal imagery, theology becomes irrelevant to man's deepest concerns. If he cannot worship God in personal as well as impersonal terms, he ends by worshiping himself, or some part of nature, or nothing at all.

Finally, just as our theological language is not complete without impersonal and personal elements, so our daily commerce with finite events requires both science and poetry. We have to see ourselves and the world through our own eyes. We are given no other window. We must interpret events either as quasi-persons to be communed with or materials for our use. We have no other way of living or feeling. We must either be interested, loving, fearing, hating toward what we meet or we must be detached from it and thereby free either to avoid it or to use it as we will. Otherwise we cannot respond to reality. But these two kinds of responses should be enough for us. By manipulating things and the world we gain some transcendence over the world and time. By loving things and the world we keep in vital relation to that which sustains us; and we are prevented from slaying that which we love. Neither the personal nor the impersonal view of reality is complete in itself; both views partake of our own finitude and limitations. But neither is the personal or impersonal view of reality entirely meaningless; both views constitute the very essence of what we are, not only in ourselves, but in our belongingness to the whole. Personal communion and its symbols, impersonal analysis and its symbols, are each legitimate ways of approaching, though never exhausting, the deep mystery of being in which our very lives are founded.

10. THE LIBERAL TRANSMISSION
OF TRADITION

To be liberal in religious life, to be oriented to novelty and experiment, is not incompatible with a deep respect for ancient religious traditions. Freedom and tradition are complementary. The care with which the religious liberal exercises and transmits his tradition should strengthen his aptitude for intellectual inquiry and bring more sharply into play his powers of analytical precision.

The primary role of tradition in any culture is the ordering and articulation of experience. Language itself is perhaps the most basic of all traditions. Its forms and meanings are given, although not in so rigid a fashion that no originality can emerge. There is a definiteness to any language which commands attention and respect if communication itself is to occur, much less if any significant novelty can take place. In the power of that formal definiteness men articulate to one another and within themselves something of the complexity of meaning inherent in the variety of their experiences. There should be no need to belabor the point that language would fail utterly in its function—would not exist—if it did not carry with it traditional images and traditional rules of usage and procedure by which a community of communication is established. The most skeptical philosopher insisting that one define his terms carefully and use them consistently is appealing not to a principle of freedom but rather to a principle of linguistic tradition. Two or more discussants must share what is traditionally given in their words before they can profitably weigh the significance of their words.

The same is true of the religious life—especially true since the objects of religious devotion are often difficult to define. Here we must depend upon more than linguistic traditions since our normal framework of linguistic meaning is scarcely adequate to the task of theological articulation. Only when language is supplemented by expressive traditions in art and worship is articulation (and thereby, communication) achieved. Men must literally help one another to religious realization by communal use of the cultural tools inherited for that purpose. And their powers of novel realization will be consequent upon, not separate from, their mastery of the given articulations of their own culture.

The vital thread of traditional expression in the arts is perhaps not adequately acknowledged in this age of artistic innovation. Northrop Frye has pointed out that the history of literary art shows a continuing preoccupation with archetypal images of the human condition. Literary creativity is not purely a fresh response of writers to the stimuli of their own times. It is rather a wrestle for significant novelty within inherited forms of literary expression and subject matter. Frye notes a parallel with the religious life in which the myths and rituals of a given culture carry the archetypal models providing the means by which the people of that culture articulate to one another their basic religious questions.[1] Meanings of any great significance are far too complex in their social and communal bearing to be generated *de novo* by the isolated individual. The natural liberal tendency to say, "Each person must achieve his own religious faith," makes sense only against the broad background of inherited tradition. The very opportunity to choose what one shall believe limits one's freedom of judgment to the few vivid and viable alternatives given in one's own time and place. Even before any sensible choice can be made, there is a prior and more fundamental task facing the individual of articulating internally what some of

[1] Northrop Frye, "The Language of Poetry," in *Explorations in Communication*, Beacon Press, 1960, pp. 43-53.

the choices and questions are, where to begin and, especially, where one is standing while one begins.

There is a danger that these elemental tasks shall be construed in too intellectual a fashion, as though a lecture about the meaning of worship were a valid substitute for the living experience. It is the unique function of art and ritual to unfold, with the impact of a current experience, the depth of past culture. Works of art and religious liturgies are not propositional arguments to be weighed intellectually, but living actions commending their truths with the persuasive force of an experienced fact. Their very vitality and powers of persuasion can raise intellectual questions and lead to study and analysis. But total involvement at the experiential level precedes and stimulates theoretical detachment, not vice versa.

The subject matter of religious articulation is theoretically not bound to any one time and place. But practically speaking it is more difficult to appropriate an alien religious tradition than to assimilate one which has helped determine one's own culture and experience. If, as I have tried to show, the religious traditions of Israel and Greece and their joining under the Christian aegis have been decisive in the formation of Western religious culture, it is reasonable to expect that these traditions continue to provide the images and archetypes for the liberal's questioning and thinking. Our traditions are not dogmas in and of themselves; they are simply our native religious language. The real value of this language in comparison to alternatives can best be estimated only after we have learned to speak it well. In this respect, the liberal church has a primary and truly basic task: it has to present via the media of ritual drama, story and artistic celebration the particular images of religious encounter and religious hope which belong to the Hellenic and Judeo-Christian traditions. Raw experience is a mystery which persistently eludes our powers of expression. It is a fire burning within the individual, ever seeking some outlet, desiring communicative expression and self-definition. One's church should be the first place in one's life where something of the richness, the terror, and the ultimate hopes of the human condition are articulated. Articulations may occur as

questions or answers, doubts or affirmations. Nothing should
be considered exempt from skeptical inquiry of the individual.
But the articulations themselves in the setting of the church,
as in the arts, are not to be presented or construed primarily
as propositional arguments awaiting testing and verification.
Rather they are ritual, dramatic, musical or narrative occasions
in which essential meanings are conveyed through the very
form and immediacy of the media. They are actions and re-
enactments primarily, and only secondarily are they ideas and
hypotheses. Stated more precisely, one unique function of the
church lies in its acts of worship. People seek together to
commune directly with that reality which they believe sus-
stains their lives and gives meaning to their existence. To substitute analysis and discourse for worship is to miss the religious moment and compromise the very character of the
church.

The preservation and presentation of traditional forms and
ideas of worship insures that there shall be definite articulation
of individual religious feeling and not an endless and unfulfilled groping. This task is not to be construed as antiquarian.
The past is never alive except in relation to contemporary
experience. The past comes into the present only as it provides
the resonance for an activity, feeling, and stimulus occurring
contemporaneously. This musical metaphor is singularly apt.
The intensity of current events may cause people's feelings to
vibrate as the strings of a musical instrument. They will vibrate
rapidly but with a thin and pathetic sound, with difficult
strainings and painful shatterings, unless these motions of
time and circumstance occur in relation to some resonance
chamber of the past. The arts and the church provide the inherited yet malleable shapes of cultural resonance chambers.
The church will sound most richly when it is not stuffed with
rigid dogmas, with old rags of doctrine in its inner spaces. But
these inner spaces are not infinite or unbounded. They are
formed by the shapes of ancient stories, remembered patterns
of human action, words, songs and figures reminiscent of ancient times. These lend their resonance and tonality to whatever contemporary event may move through its walls. The

church's newest concerns are treasured no less than its oldest memories, but the treasuring of either old or new is dependent upon their mutual coexistence.

Such a view of the church recognizes the psychological value of relating the individual to a broad community of the living and the dead. He is lifted out of the isolating belief that his ecstasies and agonies are peculiar to himself or to his immediate location in time and space. He is put into a relationship which is at once historical, concrete, in time, and also eternal, essential, and beyond time.

Thus, while the church is also a house of study, a place of inquiry, investigation and argument, it is primarily a house of worship. Worship is its most native emphasis; intellectual analysis is always consequent upon the reality of its worship, never a substitute for it. The dramatic and celebrative element should dominate and the element of inquiry should be secondary.

We are speaking here of emphases, not of mutually exclusive functions. It is my contention that the habit of critical analysis is most readily stimulated when the celebrative and ritual functions of the church are kept fresh and imaginative, where they are not allowed to atrophy by unbroken repetition. The mind is awakened by the deepening of the feelings and dulled by the failure to touch the depth of feeling. In this respect the arts are primary tools and allies of living religion; and the very health of the intellect is dependent upon the vigor of the arts working through the realm of worship.

The intellect also has its own unique life which in our day is most carefully guarded by the ethos of the university. The university complements the church in the relative emphasis given to the dramatic and the celebrative on the one hand, and the propositional and analytical on the other. The university is primarily a house of study and only secondarily a place of worship or of dramatic confrontation with human values. A house of study leans toward the objective and the impersonal, toward the realm of theoretical detachment.

Such is the university's primary responsibility, but not its only responsibility. The university also expects and hopes that it will foster a living, existential encounter between students and teachers and various cultural and religious values, not only through its formal academic rituals but also through its class-rooms and laboratories, its festivals of music and the arts, and its faculty conferences and administrative boards. No student has experienced the full range of possible education until he has moved into some immediate identification with the glory latent in his academic subject matter. But the unique spirit of the university is the habit of detachment from the exper-ienced enthusiasm and of objective examination of antecedents, consequences, and implications. In this respect the university is ever the complement and ally of the church, for the univer-sity is capable of providing tools for the analysis and purifica-tion of ecclesiastical activities. Conversely the church is the ally of the university by perpetuating with existential vitality and immediacy, the very questions and affirmations which the university seeks to understand and refine. The church articu-lates, celebrates and bears witness to a sustaining reality and, in doing so, raises many questions. The university inquires, ana-lyzes and tests any number of claims concerning sustaining real-ities and comes upon many answers. Thus the church and the university share each other's functions; but there should be no confusion about the primary emphasis of each.

By and large, the universities are not confused. They are reticent about favoring any one system of belief, though per-haps too reticent to enter as freely as they might the realm of celebration akin to worship. The liberal church, being fre-quently unsure about the meaning of worship, is confused. All too often it becomes a pale and ineffectual imitation of the uni-versity. It claims to be a clearing house for the analysis of any and all values rather than the celebrant of a body of given val-ues. Those who know firsthand of the complexities of univer-sity life and work cannot help but be amused or affronted by the pretensions of liberal churches claiming to function as uni-versities. One hour on Sunday plus an occasional class or dis-cussion group may be legitimate study activities; but they do not approach the fullness either of religion or of scholarship.

⌐   To be in the church, to preach or receive its sermons and to join in its worship is to participate in an objective spiritual heritage. To be in a liberal church is also to be free with respect to that heritage—free to appropriate what appears to be its contemporary relevance and free to raise questions and seek reform. In all that I have said about tradition, I presuppose its *liberal* transmission; I assume that religion does not necessitate a finality of dogma, but should possess the continuing energy to search for new ways and new expressive forms. It should be based on a spiritual substance which underlies and stimulates all our free probings and which supports us when we fail as well as when we succeed. That substance, inherited from the past, guides us into religious articulateness and connects us with the history of our own religious experiences. In the interplay between heritage and freedom we discover the meaning of the liberal transmission of tradition.

The biblical heritage is not a single creed demanding belief, but a challenge to all men who seek religious affirmation. There is a solid core to this challenge, and there are contrasting elements surrounding it. At the core is a group of poems, speeches and stories in which the whole of creation is understood to be under the lordship of a power at once loving and merciful toward all creatures and yet far transcendent over the grasp of any creature including man. As William James put it, this religious vision is of "the human surrounding the brutal." It is a vision in which the mystery and austerity of the Greek or existentialist outlook have a limited place but in which the deepest relationship to reality is one of rejoicing and loving trust. It is a vision involving man's person-to-person transaction with the depth of being which is called by many names, yet no name does any more than point to that which it does not fully comprehend. Yet, finally, it is a vision in which the mysterious heart of existence seeks out man and gives to him, in spite of all his weakness, resistance, and malice, the never-failing hope of a loving and redeemed issue to the course of his life.

I trust that I have presented the actual challenge of biblical faith non-dogmatically. The liberal church does not require a literal adherence to the Scriptures but rather it hopes that some such spirit of affirmation and optimism will receive celebrative expression and be available to its people for their articulation and concern.

As we have already seen, the biblical heritage includes proto-existentialist elements, especially in the Wisdom Literature and in the tragic narratives of the Crucifixion. The Bible is not one pure strain of religious witness but a composite of affirmation and denial in varying imageries, some of which point (in content, not in historical association) toward the Hellenic heritage in Western culture. We need to broaden the conception of what is "biblical" and, while acknowledging the central core, attend also to the variations in archetypes. And although we have not inherited directly from Greece any modes of worship which we can naturally and easily assume, we have her art, her drama and literature as a reminder of her profound influence on all our history and thought patterns. Liberal churchmen should carefully inject into the activity of the church the varied legacy of classical Greece, her celebration of natural beauty, her rationalism, her sense for the tragic, and her stoical courage. The re-establishment of modern man's alliance with Greece, as we have already pointed out, is facilitated by the rise and growth of modern existentialism. Thus the archetypes of our culture are not entirely harmonious. And if these archetypes enshrine the inner conflicts which today we feel in existentialist terms, they help to make those conflicts manifest and at least potentially manageable.

The optimism of the liberal, deeply fortified by his biblical heritage, is ever challenged by the tragic humanism of his Greek heritage and its occasional counterparts in the Bible. The anchorage of hope is not untroubled and should never claim to be. But the fact remains that the great gift of the biblical heritage lies bright before our eyes, preserved and transmitted, however imperfectly, through the living church. It represents the communion of all those diverse and often conflicting believers who have been touched by its haunting challenge, who have made some of its ways their ways, who have adopted some of its prayers and who have taken one another in marriage, christened their children, and been received at their death under its many blessings. This is the liberal church in its most distinct and historical flavor, in its unique personality, going far beyond that shapeless definition as simply the body of those who inquire freely together on religious matters.

The second aspect of the function of the liberal church is to serve, as we have said, as a house of inquiry and experiment. It is a religious institution of free men who freely question and alter their heritage. This principle has a number of specific implications. First and most obviously, one is a member not by virtue of subscribing to any one dogma—or any set of doctrines. One's major relation to the heritage may be largely critical. Certainly it need not be one of total acquiescence. Secondly, one does not deny *oneself* when one enters the church. He brings with him his own peculiar stock of powers and weaknesses, his own experiences and biases, everything that has either attracted or repelled him anywhere in life. He brings himself as an offering, and if what he must offer seems to run counter to the heritage of the church, so be it; let the offering be made without fear. This means that the objective and historical core of church faith is constantly in dialogue with changing times, just as every man carries on an inner dialogue between his own biographical past and his unfolding present. If this dialogue takes place with vigor both present and past, modern existence and heritage are transformed and renewed within the individual and the church. The church need not be jealous for the sanctity of any one doctrine no matter how carefully worded. It is much more important that each worshiper be as honest as possible with himself and with tradition, turning ultimately to the religious hope that the good which was appropriate to former times can be renewed, transformed and made manifest in our own times. The liberal church trusts that its heritage is a continuing challenge to haunt the human spirit. It trusts that all of its great moments, especially the central moment of the life and death of Christ, constitute a reality which every man must come to terms with, even if the "coming to terms" is largely negative. As long as the rejection is a considered one, is the result of deep experience and soul-searching, then for such a man the church has done its work in a most significant way. Only when the church is utterly ashamed of its heritage and must flee away from it on principle, is the church denying itself and ceasing to be. The person and image of Christ are not gods to be worshiped; they are realities to be encountered and pitted against our reality and they demand of us and our children serious concern. We must face these realities lest we fall into an existence which is less than human. What that reality shall finally mean for us is a function of God's guidance and our own decision. It can not be the subject of arbitrary imposition by any one of the churches or by any person in them. And even though the reality of God in any man's life has grown dim or has vanished altogether, still the dramatic witness of the church's heritage and substance must be non-coercively available to all. Thus one is free to make decisions which in a narrower liberalism could not be made for lack of substance and alternatives.

I am bold to counsel the leaders of the liberal church—the ministers and all laymen in responsible positions—to be mindful of this obligation. Their own personal tastes and decisions relating to theological matters are unimportant compared to their duty as guardians of an ancient institution. They must make available to future generations that basic Jewish and Christian substance from which the power of the church has arisen. They are also under obligation to broaden the conception of heritage by relating the church's life to non-biblical sources of spiritual insight. They are free to teach and celebrate more than the Bible; they are not free to teach and celebrate less.

Finally it should be said that no doctrine or body of teaching is in itself any automatic guarantee of virtue. That is, an atheist may be ethically more acute and socially more productive than a believer. But this fact proves neither the validity of unbelief nor the fallacy of belief. Men differ in their powers as well as in their beliefs. A man must be free to believe even though a more acute and admirable man does not. There can be no promise, "If you believe as I do your life will be like mine." Religion is not a technique. There are good men and weak men, righteous men and evil men in every church and outside every church. And although the strongest faith should and does have a great effect on the believer's life, the effect cannot be transferred by transferring the belief. It must be acknowledged that the penetration of grace is an utterly mysterious thing which no man nor church controls and which can fail the instant either men or churches claim to know its secret.

In short, we cannot conclude that, because wonderful people live apart from the spiritual substance of the church, the church is irrelevant. The substance of the heritage is given to us who care for the church as a trust to be guarded, reformed, and transmitted. It demands that we be honest and free with ourselves and our neighbors, openly confessing our doubts as well as our assurances. It demands that we bring to bear in our religious pilgrimage anything good or true or beautiful which we happen to find in or outside of the tradition. The final issue of all our efforts is happily not ours to decide.

11. WORSHIP IN THE LIBERAL CHURCH

The interplay of heritage and freedom in liberal religion can be illustrated by looking at the procession of ritual embodied in the calendar of the church year. The calendar is normally divided into three major festivals: Thanksgiving, Christmas and Easter. Each of these festivals is coordinated with important turning points in the seasonal calendar: Thanksgiving and the harvest, Christmas and the winter solstice, Easter and the spring equinox. A complete freedom of experiment with respect to the particular subject matter to be embodied in the celebrations of the calendar is an indispensable part of the liberal religious spirit. What follows are my own suggestions concerning the possible content of an annual calendar of liberal worship. The scope of this calendar will be such as to allow a far greater range and variety of concrete liturgical and artistic procedure than is here presented. The basic shape of the calendar is such as to convey, through every variation in detail, the decisive religious elements upon which Western culture is founded. A diligent care for the ritual celebration of the rhythms of the calendar gives promise that the religious impact of the church will be felt non-cognitively and artistically as well as verbally and cognitively. Hopefully the church will thereby experience a rebirth of its power to help its people articulate the elemental issues of their religious pilgrimage.

Thanksgiving is a unique religious festival in that it has both a Christian and a native American origin. Its national, American flavor continues to sustain its celebration outside as well as within the church. Its focus in the home is conducive to a secular rather than ecclesiastical procedure. It is also easily available for church observance, either in the Sunday service immediately preceding its traditional Thursday date, or on Thursday, often through the medium of a union service held for the members of several congregations within a given area. Its appeal, like that of all great festivals, transcends denominational limits.

The fullness of the harvest image at the time of Thanksgiving reminds man of his indebtedness to the process of life itself. The mood of contrivance and control which must necessarily surround the producing and marketing of goods gives way to the mood of gratitude. This gratitude is not primarily motivated by some feeling of courtesy toward a benevolent reality. It comes from a more fundamental motivation, arising out of the instinct to express one's closeness to and reverence for all that sustains life. It is the instinct to love that which one uses, to rejoice in that which is humbly necessary, to offer one's own energy to assist the whole pageant of life. It is the recognition of the wonderfully varied and mutually sustaining glory of existence, as surprising in detail and harmonious in total effect as the panorama of autumn foliage. One gives thanks not to relieve an obligation but to rejoice in mutual indebtedness. It is an expression of faith that the life-sustaining conditions of indebtedness and interrelation have not withered in our barren age. Giving thanks is a way of keeping alive, as crucial as breathing. Not to be able to acknowledge the ultimate gift of life, not to be free to accept an undeserved and overflowing bounty, is in itself a sign of deep spiritual malaise, a drifting toward the illusion of self-sufficiency and the subsequent illusion of utter solitude.

It should be noted that Thanksgiving Day is not an isolated twenty-four hours of festival, but rather the climax of an entire season which begins several months earlier. In its most obvious physical beginnings, the harvest dates from the middle of August when an increased flow of fresh fruits and vegetables reaches the markets. Of greater potential religious significance is the observance of Labor Day on the first Monday in September. In the midst of the flood tide of agricultural harvest, at the end of the summer's vacation, at the beginning of the church's year and of the vocational year, we pause to celebrate the profound significance of human labor. I envisage this celebration as standing in fruitful polarity with Thanksgiving Day. On Thanksgiving men express their gratitude for goods they have been given and cannot themselves effect. On Labor Day they celebrate the *powers* that are given with which they *can* make a tangible effect; they celebrate their cooperative relationship with nature as stewards and transformers of her benefits. Therefore, I would open the new church year on the Sunday before Labor Day, all vacationists notwithstanding. The service would concentrate on the injunction in Genesis, that man should be fruitful and multiply and have dominion over the earth, and should subdue and replenish it. The fact of human labor is thus manifold in its sacramental significance. "To be fruitful and multiply" is to share with all living things their power to give birth and their cocreative energies. "To have dominion over the earth" is a peculiarly human prerogative, emphasizing the gift of human intelligence and the obligation to use it toward mutually creative ends. To "subdue and replenish" the earth combines the technological with the conservationist elements in human labor: man must bring forth his uniquely human products out of natural materials and must also protect the supply of nature's abundance from exhaustion. Thus the church year begins on a note of abundance and celebration in which human rejoicing is focused first of all on man himself and on his position of cooperative stewardship to nature. Psychologically, the date of such a festival is peculiarly advantageous, standing as it does in the pause between vacation and the resumption of the working year. From vacation it derives the perspective of leisurely reflection and the restoration of vital powers through rest and relaxation. On facing the resumption of vocational labor, it elicits a rededication of each person to realize the satisfactions and hoped-for improvements within his chosen field.

Falling almost midway between Labor Day and Thanksgiving Day is the October 12 holiday recognizing Columbus' discovery of America. Here is an opportunity to stress further dimensions of this prolonged season of abundance. The liberal church has traditionally emphasized the sacred quality of exploration and discovery. Too often religious liberalism has overstressed the conscious heroism of successful human explorers and discoverers and has not adequately recognized their humble dependence upon their forerunners, their trust in Providence, and their sense of awesome privilege and joyful indebtedness before the wonder of what they had been given to discover. Columbus is at once the first American, a local saint, and a worldwide symbol of the adventure of modern man. However, his day in October arouses little excitement among Americans above elementary school age, possibly because of our tendency to isolate holidays from the larger seasons in which they could have a significant part. Consequently, I see the hope that the liberal church might celebrate the day of the Great Discovery as an integral symbol of the abundance signalized on Labor Day and reaching its climax on Thanksgiving Day.

Whereas Columbus Day memorializes the opening of the New World, United Nations Day on October 24 is the occasion for celebrating the unity of the New and Old Worlds, if not in fact, then as an ideal yet to be fulfilled. The crowning human achievement would be the Peaceable Kingdom of the entire planet, the rule of law among all nations. Here is a potential human creation no less significant in value nor less worthy of celebration than all the richness of our natural resources and human ingenuity. The rhythm of the liberal church year could move from the relatively nationalistic focus of Columbus Day to United Nations Day as the practical expression of the age-old dream of the unity of all nations in Zion and the unity of all men as brothers under God. Hopefully it would be possible to incorporate into one's religious observance of Thanksgiving Day a recapitulation of the religious realities of Labor Day, Columbus Day, and United Nations Day, thus bringing the whole season of Thanksgiving to a distinct climax.

To see Thanksgiving as a season, not merely as a day, would also provide a medium for articulating and celebrating several other similar rhythms in human life. This season begins the year in the mood of praise and affirmation. In addition to the seasonal reference to harvest, the time of abundant harvest and restored human energy, there are the corresponding periods of the morning of each day and the youth of each life. The morning is the hour of restoration and vigorous hope. The youth is hopefully a person of unalloyed vigor and idealism who, like a bridegroom, "rejoiceth as a strong man to run a race." Furthermore, just as the year, the day, the life, begin on a note of triumph, the note of "sheer morning gladness at the brim," so should every service of worship in all seasons begin. I am indebted to Von Ogden Vogt for his insight that religion involves celebration, and that the great recurring pattern of human worship among many diverse liturgies is to begin the service on a note of praise and thanksgiving.[1]

Following the climax of the season of Thanksgiving, we come upon a point of crisis and change in the passage of the natural and liturgical season. The length of the day is waning and we move into the time of winter. The heating systems of our houses protect us from the physical discomfort of the coming cold weather, but the symbolic effect of that seasonal change is not without influence upon us. Aesthetically, the golden season of autumn deteriorates into the drab colors and stark white of winter. The growing season is at an end, the green vanishes, animals and birds are largely absent. Underlying the onset of these aesthetic contrasts are certain deeper and darker movements of the human spirit. The realization of abundance carries with it an undertone of anxiety over the inevitable diminishing that must come to all forms of power and vitality. A basic element in the human religious consciousness is a certain terror toward the inevitable movement of time and the decay and death it brings. As we have noted in our discussion of the Hellenic religious mind and its modern existentialist and biblical counterparts, the terror of time can be a source of despair. The Greeks were keenly aware of the natural beauty and abundance of their lands and seas. Their

[1] Von Ogden Vogt, *Modern Worship*, Yale University Press, 1927, chap. II, and *Art and Religion*, rev. ed., Beacon Press, 1948, chap. XV.

sense of tragedy was sharpened by the vivid contrast between the beauty of abundance and the inevitability of its total loss. The terror of time was symbolized for primitive men in the shortening of the days toward the winter solstice, in the accompanying diminution of vegetable growth and game supply and in the onset of cold weather. Paraphrasing Anaximander, it is as if nature were making us pay in full for her previous bounties, as though man were giving a just recompense for his former privileges.

The power of the Advent season with its climax at Christmas is that it introduces a sustaining note of hope into this dark period. It partially anticipates Easter by announcing the surprising news that the power of renewal is active where it is least expected—in the very setting of decline and decay. A paradox is thus made manifest: whereas the season of fullness had been the prelude to emptiness, the season of emptiness contains within it the unexpected and unlikely seed of renewal. In the dark of the year, in the dark of the night, on pastures, in mangers, in desert wanderings, rather than among the principalities and powers, we look for the new beginnings of mankind. In the Child, in children, we must finally put our trust, knowing that our own wisdom must ultimately fail, our buildings fall, our bodies wither, knowing, also, that none of these terrors shall ultimately terrify as long as there are children. We acknowledge that all mighty acts, the very salvation of the Lord extended to a waiting people, must have their beginnings in littleness. Therefore the faithful, who can see only the advent and Christmas Eve of their hopes, do not despair in the world's night. They count the angels' song of peace and goodwill as a real and sacred promise, just as the ancient Jews trusted the promises of their God even while they wandered in the wilderness or languished in captivity.

From the point of view of our religious heritage, all worship is ultimately celebration and the final religious emotion is one of affirmation and joy. However, there is a significant difference between the joy of Thanksgiving and the joy of Christmas and Easter. In the latter two seasons we emphasize with increasing intensity that overwhelmingly religious preposition, "in spite of." Christmas represents the renewal of hope in the seed, in its germinal form, in spite of evidence, both real and symbolic, of decline. Easter represents the full triumph of hope and power in spite of the complete realization of tragedy. Thanksgiving, by contrast, is a season of unalloyed affirmation, youthful in its confident vigor, like the trumpet notes of praise at the beginning of a day, a year, or a Sunday service. The Advent and Christmas season is a primary response to the onset of anxiety. The anxieties of the Advent season are analogous to the deep anxieties of the youth who suffers the first pains of mature responsibility, or to that melancholy of the intellect which can logically envisage the loss of every benefit and protection that human life has managed to build for itself. Von Ogden Vogt has called this the second major element of liturgical rhythm, when after the opening notes of praise, the congregation turns to the mood of contrition and confesses man's personal and social inadequacy. Dr. Vogt draws this analogy from the first part of Isaiah, chapter 6, where the prophet, having seen the glory of God in the temple is driven to confess, "Woe is me! for I am undone; because I am a man of unclean lips, and I dwell in the midst of a people of unclean lips: for mine eyes have seen the King, the Lord of hosts." In the darkness of Isaiah's confession he speaks of a visitation of an angel who purges his mouth with a live coal taken from the high altar. Thus is symbolized God's initiative in lifting man's despair. Similarly, the Advent season comes to a bright climax at Christmas.

There is a temptation to treat this Christmas witness of renewed hope in a Greek rather than in a biblical way. The natural and cyclical element of Christmas would be stressed rather than the divine element. We would point to the fact that every night is followed by a new dawn and every winter has its spring. The child would be largely symbolic of the comfort to be derived from the presence of the young and the encouragement manifested in the newness of all growth. The melancholy of old age would be somewhat allayed by an aesthetic appreciation of the vigor of oncoming generations. I see some such rejoicing implied in Camus' statement of the

"invincible summer" at the heart of his own suffering consciousness.

Christianity may have incorporated into Christmas some
of these more naturalistic elements. But we should not allow
them to dominate the meaning of Christmas exclusively, any
more than we should limit Easter to a spring fertility festival.
The central faith of Christmas is that of the incarnation, where
Christ is called "Immanuel," "God with us." This is an extension of the age-old trust of Israel that, in the critical and unlikely situation, God is capable of extending his sustaining
strength directly to man. The Child is presented as Holiness
incarnate. It is possible for the liberal worshiper to endorse
this symbolic meaning without making Christ an object of
idolatrous worship. This Child has emerged manifesting the
human dimension of Holiness. God far transcends man, but he
is also in man and most readily revealed through particular
men. God is revealed as incarnate in man at the humble beginnings of life as well as in its mature expression. The power of
God to reveal itself in the dark season and in the tender and
helpless vessel is a witness of his transcendence over the mere
cycles of nature, of his efficacy where men dare least to look for
it. The conventional image of a full-grown, kingly Messiah is
expanded to include God's presence in the merest child, born in
the least fertile season of the year.

Although the Jewish conception of the Messiah is thus
extended, the Jewish disclaimer of idolatry is not to be ignored.
The Child does not command our worship even though he is a
vehicle of incarnate love. We celebrate the power of the Child
to bear witness to the Creator; but prayer itself belongs to God
alone. No manifestation of holiness should be given worship
or be treated as an idol.

There is one important element of Christmas which, in
the general mood of rejoicing, is often ignored. Herod's
jealousy and his slaughter of the innocents force the Holy
Family to become refugees in a foreign land. Thus at the
very beginning of the Gospels, the note of persecuted innocence is sounded, anticipating the terrible climax of the
Crucifixion. One is reminded of the frightening contradiction

in human life, of the tendency of man to slay that which he most loves and needs. Some such sense of tragic contradiction must have assaulted Isaiah when, having seen the glory of God, his mind immediately jumped to the personal and social guilt he felt within and around him. The vision of holiness had the initial effect of underlining his own unworthiness.

It seems to me that this gap between vision and action, between an occasional glory felt or thought and a persisting sense of imperfection in human behavior, is a universal religious tension. Not unlike Isaiah, the author of Job says in his last chapter: "I have heard of thee by the hearing of the ear: but now mine eye seeth thee. Wherefore I abhor myself and repent in dust and ashes." In keeping with the terror occurring at the end of the Christmas story, we conclude that the doctrine of incarnation is not in itself adequate to all of man's religious needs. The shadow of tragedy hangs as a continuing threat over every manifestation of hope. Even the divine dimension of Christmas, if isolated from the larger range of the biblical heritage, may lead to a tragic melancholy.

Perhaps this melancholy is nowhere so devastating as when it occurs in the very loveliness of the spring season. The leap of spring with all its glory is then construed as the material for eventual decline or tragedy. Thus T. S. Eliot could characterize April as "the cruellest month." In the very radiance of spring, during the ecstatic blossoming of the promise, the onset of tragedy can be most devastating. Suffering and loss are never so terrible as when they come to the young, or to those who have moved into the fullness of their powers. Whitman relates the poignancy of Lincoln's death to the heart-rending contrast of lilacs blooming in the dooryard. He has to mourn "with ever-returning spring." The great triumph of the resurrection of the world in spring is not that it is beautiful and cheerful and altogether invigorating, but rather, that we carry into those exquisite days the knowledge of all pain and tragedy, seeking, in the juxtaposition of life and death, the courage to accept both together.

This means that Easter requires Good Friday. What could be merely an innocuous spring festival, takes on the depth and somberness of the struggle of life and hope with death and despair. This season is *the* season of Jesus Christ. It is the acute recognition of the fact that all that is most exquisitely creative in life endures endless hostility and carries, in the form of the suffering servant, the sorrow of the world. There are helpless mothers who grieve for these fearful sacrifices; and there are frightened disciples who flee for their lives haunted by fear and guilt. There are anonymous bloodthirsty crowds who demand to be entertained by death. There are soldiers and guards who must shield their own sensibilities from any true realization of the crimes they are forced to commit. There are old men crafty in the perpetration of fraud, never revealing to the mobs they inspire the emptiness in their own endless scheming. Good Friday sums up all that ever tempted any Greek or existentialist to despair and requires mankind to look, as in a mirror, and "behold the Man." Love is seen in its most terrible aspect; the love that must suffer and be crucified, the love that an impatient Judas could not accept but had to blot out of his consciousness as a prelude to taking his own life.

Easter is the trumpet call in the morning of this dark night. Easter proclaims, though man and death have done their worst, that all is not ended, that the ending is better than the beginning. Easter is an ineffable compassion. It is the compassion of Christ toward his murderers; the compassion of the disciples toward the engines of the state, but more especially toward one another and toward themselves. The worst having happened, and that worst having ingrained in them a fierce guilt for their cowardice and flight, they rose up in the morning, returned to Jerusalem, rejoiced in the temple, and went out to teach men how to rejoice with ever-returning spring.

Out of every misguided attempt to interpret these shocking and wonderful events some truth is continually available. The world is not such that it must condemn man to eternal night. In biblical form, God is merciful and ever ready to forgive, "Thou hast put off my sack-cloth and girded me with gladness." Man is not such that he must carry to his grave an unbreakable scorn and grievance for his sorrow-laden life. He can learn to forgive his Creator for the miseries of creation even as he learns that his Creator suffers with and is ready to renew all creatures. This is the Good News that the celebration of Easter teaches the mind and injects into the heart and nerves. This is the last and greatest Passover which, from ancient times, belongs to that long procession of passovers that the people of the Old Testament saw shining in their wilderness, filling their lives with hope.

As the festival of compassion, Easter and the Easter season constitute man's ultimate defense against the threat of despair. When a person suffers, he is not able in his internally diminished state to take comfort from the fact that there are external realms of power and glory still operating. One cannot ask a sick man to be comforted by the presence of a vigorous and healthy visitor at his bedside. The patient may become all the more melancholy through witnessing the sharp contrast. Similarly, Job does not complete the religious cycle by seeing a vision of God's glory and then by repenting in dust and ashes. Beyond repentance, beyond humility, is the desperate need for compassionate love and all its restorative powers. Job might also have said, "I have seen thy terror and thy glory, but I need also thy compassion."

Easter is that witness of compassion, affirming the mystery that God in Christ and God in all men suffers with us in our tragedies and is that power of renewal rising with us beyond tragedy. This is not a literal pronouncement. It does not pretend to be an affirmation of immortality nor any claim to understand scientifically or exactly the meaning of the resurrection story. It is a symbolic affirmation that the Creator, the center and source of life, that mysterious something which religious men are led to praise, enters into our tragedies and provides the power of healing and rejuvenation. There is no way to understand this faith mechanically. The annual celebration of Easter is nevertheless the tangible, particular, historical witness of the faith. Furthermore, the experience of the witness through its communal liturgical form in the church transcends in possible meanings this, or any other, verbal analysis. The immediacy and depth of the festival is there to stimulate our thought and action; but no thought and action is adequate definition of the living community and its worship.

To the worshiper, Easter is the mysterious yet ever meaningful reinvigoration of his hopes and actions. It is analogous to the wisdom of mature experience which moves through pain to new strength. It is analogous to the burgeoning fullness of the year beyond the winter's dark. It is analogous to the climax of any service of worship when, after the initial praise and the consequent confession, there is a renewal of the sense of immediate holiness and a rededication of human powers. With Easter the year is thus complete. Man moves forward to his labors as the fields ripen and bring forth their fruit. The circle of the season turns and once again we approach the time of Thanksgiving with its celebration of man's powers and discoveries and its rejoicing in the overflowing bounty of the world.

Perhaps this age-old rhythm of Thanksgiving, Christmas and Easter with its Jewish parallels in the New Year, the Day of Atonement, Hanukkah and Passover is also reflected in the more stately rhythms of history itself. For nations and cultures there are times of fullness, of tragedy, of renewal. It may be that the mood of near-despair and the courage of desperation which has fallen upon the Western world still has many decades to run its course and worse crises may be in store. It may be that in the immediate future no rational system will be safe against the onslaughts of impersonal events, that all logical and verbal meaning will be dissolved in the minds of many men and women of good will. If this must be, I shall need the community of my church all the more during the festive seasons of the year. I shall need a church where I can continue to celebrate Thanksgiving, a church where I can sing the lovely songs in recognition of the incarnation, a church where the harrowing and wonderful drama of death and resurrection can be reenacted before my eyes and restored in my heart. New words, new concepts will come in time, through the nourishment of the wordless faith.

This is the house we build and guard for our children, in which the mighty hope is strangely enshrined. God grant that it may be given to them to rejoice and be glad in it.

INDEX

Abraham, 67, 78, 79, 81, 94
Absolute truth, existentialist critique of 20, 62
Abstraction, existentialist critique of, 21, 62
Achaeans, 56
Adam, 66
Advent, 121
Aegistheus, in Sartre's *The Flies,* 20
Agamemnon, 57
Anaximander, 121
Anthropomorphism, 93, 94, 98, 101-103, 111
Aphrodite, 54
Aquinas, 84
Argos, 20
Aristotle, 58-60, 69, 84
Art, 19, 42, 106-110, 116
Atheism, 114
Athena, 55, 58
Athenians, 58
Atomism, 99
Aulis, 57

Barrett, William, 27, 61
Being, concept of, 18, 20, 23, 59, 60, 61, 98
Benjamin, 77
Bergson, Henri, 85
Biblical tradition, 48, 64-92 passim, 114; as poetry, 95-98; divine-human communion, 95, 98-102
Buber, Martin, 46, 95

Cadmus, 51
Calendar of liberal worship, 116-127
Camus, Albert, 28-39, 51, 55, 58, 62, 63, 73, 81, 90, 122; *The Fall,* 21, 28-30, 33, 74; *The Myth of Sisyphus,* 31, 32, 34, 36; *The Plague,* 32, 33; *The Rebel,* 34, 38; Nobel Prize acceptance speech, 35, 36; *Summer in Algiers,* 37; *Nuptials,* 37

Chaos, in Greek mythology, 52
Charities (Greek mythology), 54
Charybdis, 55
Christianity, 2, 8, 11, 23, 24, 36, 38, 41, 48, 83-89, 123
Christmas, 116, 121, 127
Church, liberal doctrine of, 1, 2; as "substance," 2, 7 ff.; as "method," 2; in relation to its heritage, 42, 49, 107-115
Clytemnestra, 57
Columbus Day, 118, 119
Communion with the Divine, 95, 98-102
Concern (Quaker), 46
Contributionism, 100
Covenant theology, 65-72
Creation, Jewish doctrine of, 65, 103, 118; Greek doctrine of, 51
Creativity, 86-91; in existentialism, 11
Creon, 58
Crucifixion, 83, 93, 112, 123
Culture and religion, 7-9, 44, 45
Cyclopes, 53
Cynicism, 62

Dante, 47
Day of Atonement, 127
Destiny, Greek concept of, 56, 57; Jewish concept of, 67-69, 71, 77
Devil, in MacLeish's *J.B.,* 75
Dialogue of past and present, 108, 113
Dignity of man, concept of, 10
Disgust, Sartre's concept of, 75
Dostoevski, 19, 21, 61

Earth Mother, 52
Easter, 116, 121, 124-127
Ecclesiastes, 73, 74
Education in liberal religion, 12
Electra, 57; in Sartre's *The Flies,* 19
Eliot, T. S., 124
Emerson, Ralph Waldo, 25, 26
Enlightenment, The, 13, 24

Erebus, 52

Eros, 53

Esau, 67, 68

Essentialism, 10, 17, 59; in Plato, 17, 59, 60, 88

Estrangement, Jewish doctrine of, 66, 67, 89; Greek doctrine of, 57, 58, 66

Eurynome, 54

Eve, 66

Existentialism, 9, 11, 16-26, 42, 48, 62, 75, 111, 125; and freedom, 5, 14, 19-25; and pathos, 11, 20, 26, 80-82; and the dignity of man, 22, 33; metaphysical, 23; Biblical, 73 ff., 83, 112; Greek, 51, 60, 64, 112

Fall, the myth of the, 65-67

Feeling, Whitehead's concept of, 100, 101

Fertility, in Greek religion, 52, 53, 55

Festivals. See Calendar of liberal worship

Forgiveness as a theological concept, 80, 81, 87-91, 125, 126

Freedom, 1, 3, 5, 14, 21; of inquiry, 2; in Christianity and Judaism, 2, 80; in religious education, 12, 114; existential concept of, 16, 19, 20, 25, 32

Frost, Robert, 41

Frye, Northrop, 106

Furies, 54

Gaer, Joseph, 65 n.

Gaia, 52, 53

Genesis, 65, 67, 77, 78, 118

Good Friday, 124

Goya, Francisco, The Disasters of the War, 22

Grace of God, 4, 8, 9, 11, 115

Greek culture, 51-63; the natural world, 38, 48, 51, 120, 122; the tragic vision, 48, 57, 84, 120; hubris, 57; moderation, 58, 59-62; reason, 59, 60-62, 69, 70; proto-existentialism, 51, 60, 64; and the liberal church, 107, 111, 112

Guilt, existentialist concept of, 24, 30, 33

Hanukkah, 127

Hartshorne, Charles, 100

Hegel, 17

Hell, concept of, in Sartre's No Exit, 20

Heraclitus, 61, 85

Herod, 123

Hesiod, Theogany, 52 ff., 57

History, 43, 48, 108, 127

Holy Spirit, 13

Homer, 56

Hopkins, Gerard Manley, 97

Hours (Greek mythology), 54

Hubris, 57

Humanism, 9, 30, 35, 38, 48, 71; Greek, 59, 60

Humanity as a religious concept, 71

Hydra, 53

Idolatry, 41, 47, 103, 123

Immortality, 63

Incarnation, 87-91, 123

Intellect, 9, 10; in existentialism, 17, 31; and worship, 108, 109

Isaac, 78, 79

Isaiah, 97, 103, 122, 124

Israel, in the myth of Jacob's wrestling, 68

J.B. (play by MacLeish), 75, 80

Jacob, 67-69, 77, 78, 81, 103

James, William, 85, 111

Jason, 51

Jaspers, Karl, 17 n,. 18, 19, 23, 31, 32

Jesus Christ, 79, 81, 83, 84, 88, 90-92, 104, 113, 114, 123, 125

Job, 74, 75, 78, 94, 126; Book of, 74, 123

Joseph, 67, 76-78, 81, 103

Judah, 77, 78

Judaism, 41, 64-72; covenant theology, 65 ff.; doctrine of creation, 65; doctrine of estrangement, 66, 67; and existentialism, 73 ff.

Judas, 125

Judeo-Christian tradition, 40, 41, 80, 107, 114

Kaddish, 69

Kafka, Franz, The Castle, 74; The Trial, 75

Kant, Immanuel, 84

Kierkegaard, Soren, 16-18, 23, 26, 31, 32, 61

Kore, 52

Kourotrophos, 52

Kronos, 54

Labor Day, 117, 118

Language, theological, 93 ff.; and the
    arts, 106, 107
Lermontov, 30
Levi Issac, Rabbi of Berditshev, 69
Liberalism, reform, 107-127; and the
    concept of novelty, 93, 105, 107, 111;
    and the university, 110; and its heri-
    tage, 111-115; and the critical spirit,
    113
Liberalism, sectarian, 7 ff., 21, 24, 26,
    40, 48, 83; nineteenth century, 3, 4,
    14; concept of the "Dignity of Man,"
    10; of Clamence in Camus' *The Fall,*
    29; Camus' Challenge to, 38; its
    Greek roots, 60, 61; its Biblical roots,
    70, 71, 81, 90
Lincoln, Abraham, 124
Logical positivism, 10
Luther, Martin, 4

MacLeish, Archibald, *J.B.,* 75, 76, 80,
    81, 87
Man, doctrine of, 5, 9, 10; nineteenth
    century liberal, 4; Greek, 56, 57;
    Jewish, 66 ff.; existentialist, 5
Materialism, in early Greek culture, 52
Medea, 57
Melancholy, 37, 124; Greek, 38, 51, 55,
    56, 58, 62, 63, 83, 120; Jewish, 73-
    75
Melville, Herman, 25, 26
Menelaus, 56
Messiah, 123
Method of liberalism, 1, 2
Mnemosyne, 54
Moby Dick, 26
Moderation, 34, 37, 55, 58, 59-62;
    "Golden Mean," 58
Monism, 84, 85
Moses, 67, 81, 94, 103
Murray, Gilbert, 58, 61
Muses, 54
Mysticism, 43
Myth, anthropomorphism, 93, 94, 98,
    101-103; Greek, 51 ff.; Jewish, 65 ff.;
    in literature, 106

New Testament, 73, 81
Nietzsche, 17, 23, 61
Nihilism, 24, 28, 32, 34, 62
No Exit, 20

Noah, 79
Novelty, and reform liberalism, 93, 105,
    107, 111

Odysseus, 55, 58
Odyssey, The, 55, 56
Oedipus, 57, 58
Old Testament, 32, 68, 76-78, 87, 88,
    94, 126
Olympian, pantheon, 52; religion, 58
Olympianism, 44 ff.
Oresteia, The, 57
Orestes in Sartre's *The Flies,* 19, 20, 22
Organism, philosophy of, 99-101
Orthodoxy, 1, 3; Christian, 2, 4, 6; in
    liberalism, 14, 45
Ouranos, 53

Pacifism, 33
Pandora, 58
Pantheon, Olympian, 52
Pascal, 62
Passover, 126, 127
Pathos, 11, 20, 26, 33, 125, 126; Greek,
    53; slaughter of the innocents, 123
Paul, 81
Peaceable Kingdom, 119
Peirce, Charles, 85
Permissiveness, in liberalism, 3, 12
Persuasion, Whitehead's concept of, 86
Phaeacians, 56
Pharaoh, 94
Philosophical theology, 84
Picasso, Pablo, 47
Plagues of Egypt, 94
Plato, 54, 64, 69, 84; essentialism of,
    17, 59, 60, 88
Pluralism, 85, 89
Poetry, 95-98, 101, 104
Poseidon, 55
Pragmatism, 42
Prayer, 98, 99, 101, 102
Pre-established harmony, doctrine of, 13
Prometheus, 54, 57, 66
Protestantism, 4, 13, 14
Psalms, poetry of, 97

Quakers, 46

Rationalism, existentialist attack on, 16,
    17, 18; Greek, 51, 59, 60

Reason, Greek view of, 59, 60-62, 69
Rebellion, 34
Redemption, 86-89, 90, 91
Reductionism, in poetry and science, 96
Religious free market, 44 ff.
Resurrection, 79, 124, 126
Rich, Adrienne, 44
Ritual. *See* Worship

Salvation, 70, 122
Sarah, 67
Sartre, Jean-Paul, 19-21, 26, 75; *The Flies,* 19, 22; *No Exit,* 20
Saturn. *See* Kronos
Sayers, Dorothy, 47
Schleiermacher, Friedrich, 7
Science, existentialism critique of, 18, 19, 21, 42; liberal faith in, 18, 60, 104; and monistic philosophy, 85; problem of reductionism, 96
Scylla, 55
Sin, original, 4, 11, 13, 24; myth of the Fall, 65-67
Sirens, 55
Sisyphus, 31, 32
Skepticism, 62
Socrates, 59
Spinoza, 84
Spontaneity, philosophical concept of, 85, 86, 90, 91, 100, 102
Substance, of liberalism, 1, 2, 4, 7 ff., 27
Suffering servant, 76, 77-81, 88-91, 125
Symbolism, 66, 78, 79; Biblical, 93 ff., 126
Syncretism, 44

Tartarus, 52-54
Thanksgiving, 116-120, 122, 127
The Flies, 19, 22
Thebans, 51
Theism, 9, 38; Greek, 59
Themis, 54, 59
Theologia Crucis, 36, 39
Tillich, Paul, 62, 98
Titans, 53 ff.
Tragedy, Greek vision of, 48, 57, 120, 122; Melville's concept of, 26
Transcendence, 23, 69, 98, 103, 123

"Underground Man" (of Dostoevski), 21, 61
Unfulfilled seeking, 46 ff., 108
United Nations Day, 119
University, its relation to the liberal church, 110

Vogt, Von Ogden, 120, 122
Voltaire, 11

Warfare of the gods in Greek myth, 53-55, 66
Whitehead, A. N., 85, 86, 100, 104
Whitman, Walt, 124
Wieman, H. N., 86
Wisdom literature, 74, 112
Worship, 12, 42; and poetry, 96-98; as prayer, 98, 99, 101, 102; as mystery, 103; and the liberal church, 108, 109, 110; calendar of, 116-127

Zeus, 52, 54 ff., 66; in Sartre's *The Flies,* 20, 22